Credit Card Mastery

Discover In 3 Days How to Get

A 700+ Credit Score, Protect Your Credit From

Scammers And DIY Credit Repair Strategies

To Boost Your Credit

By

Michael Ezeanaka

www.MichaelEzeanaka.com

Copyright ©2020

All rights reserved. Except as permitted under the U.S. Copyright Act of 1976, the scanning, uploading and distribution of this book via the Internet or via any other means without the express permission of the author is illegal and punishable by law. Please purchase only authorized electronic editions, and do not participate in or encourage electronic piracy of copyrighted material.

Disclaimer

This publication is designed to provide competent and reliable information regarding the subject matter covered. However, it is sold with the understanding that the author is not engaged in rendering investment or other professional advice. Laws and practices often vary from state to state and country to country and if investment or other expert assistance is required, the services of a professional should be sought. The author specifically disclaims any liability that is incurred from the use or application of the contents of this book.

Please, leave a review for this book on Amazon

Table of Contents

Copyright ©2020 2

Disclaimer 3

Introduction 8

Chapter 1 11

   History and Evolution of Consumer Credit 11

      The Need for a Credit Rating System 12

      Types of Consumer Credit 12

Chapter 2 14

   How to Read, Review and Understand Your Credit Report 14

      What is a credit report, exactly? 14

      What are the benefits of credit reporting? 15

      How can you request for copies of your credit report? 16

      What if there are inaccuracies or incomplete information in your credit report? ... 17

Chapter 3 19

   Understanding Your Credit Score 19

      The FICO Score 19

      How FICO Scores are Calculated 19

      What's a Good FICO Score? 20

      The FICO Score Range 20

      The Importance of a Good Credit Score 21

      Downside of having a low credit score 22

      What to do if you have no FICO Score 24

      How to achieve a 700+ credit score 24

Chapter 4 26

   Monitoring Credit Reports and Credit Scores 26

      What are credit-monitoring services? 26

      How to check your credit score 26

      Hard and Soft Credit Inquiries 27

      Types of monitoring services available 27

Chapter 5 29

   The VantageScore Model 29

      What is a good VantageScore? 29

      VantageScore Ranges Explained 29

      How VantageScore calculates your credit score 29

      Differences between the FICO and VantageScore Models 30

Please, leave a review for this book on Amazon

Chapter 6 32

Factors That Impact Your Credit Rating 32

Payment History 32
Credit Utilization 33
Age of Accounts 34
Credit Mix 35
Recent Credit History 35
The Bottomline 36

Chapter 7 38

Factors That Do Not Affect Your Credit Score 38

Chapter 8 40

Credit Cards 40

How Credit Cards Work (Consumer Side) 40
How Credit Cards Work (Business Side) 40
Credit Card Versus Line of Credit 41
Cash Advances 42
Billing and Payment 42
Credit Card Pros and Cons 43
Types of Credit Cards 46
1. Vanilla credit cards 46
2. Reward Cards 47
3. Student credit cards 50
4. Charge cards 50
5. Secured credit cards 51
6. Sub-prime credit cards 51
7. Prepaid cards 52
8. Limited purpose cards 52
9. Business credit cards 53
Basic Features of Credit Cards 53
Factors to Consider When Choosing a Credit Card 55
Ways to Avoid a Finance Charge on Your Credit Card 57

Chapter 9 59

How To Climb The Credit Card Ladder 59

Tier 1 59
Student cards 59
Basic or secured cards 59
Subprime cards 60
Tier 2 60
Tier 2 Cards Worth Taking a Look At 61
Choosing and using a Tier 2 Card 63
Tier 3 63
Tier 4 64

Please, leave a review for this book on Amazon

Tier 5 65

Chapter 10 66

Business Credit Cards 66

What are business credit cards and what makes them different? 66

Personal vs. business: Which card should you choose? 68

Types of Business Cards 69

How to get a business credit card 70

What you need to secure a quick approval 71

What transactions could the business credit card be used for? 71

Chapter 11 73

Credit Card Balance Transfer 73

Balance Transfer in a Nutshell 73

When Should You Do a Balance Transfer? 73

Pros and Cons of Balance Transfer 74

Chapter 12 75

How to Protect Your Credit Card from Identity Theft 75

How identity theft can ruin your credit score 75

Ways to avoid becoming an identity theft victim 75

Chapter 13 79

Do-It-Yourself Credit Repair Strategies 79

Here are some of the simplest ones that you can do by yourself 79

Chapter 14 86

Biggest Credit Mistakes and How to Avoid Them 86

Chapter 15 92

Start-up Funding Sources 92

1. Bootstrapping Your Business 92

Growing Your Money Through Bootstrapping 92

Pros and Cons of Bootstrapping 93

2. Crowdfunding 94

Types of Crowdfunding 94

Pros and Cons of Crowdfunding 95

3. Angel Investors 96

Pros and Cons of Angel Investors 97

4. Venture Capital 99

Pros and Cons of Venture Capital 100

5. Business Incubators and Accelerators 101

Pros And Cons of Business Incubators and Accelerators 102

Conclusion 104

Please, leave a review for this book on Amazon

Please, leave a review for this book on Amazon

Introduction

So many people do not fully understand the power of credit. It is a very potent weapon that has the power to do good or bad depending on how it's applied by the end user. In order to fully understand how credit works (so as to position yourself to take full advantage of it), one needs to grasp the fundamental concept of a credit score.

A credit score is not just a number. It could be your ticket to a quick loan approval, low interest rates, access to exclusive airport lounges, and even free plane rides.

On the other hand, institutions and individuals can also use those same numbers to reject your loan applications and give you unfavorable deals. Such will be the case if you have a bad credit score.

This book aims to help you achieve and maintain good credit rating whilst making you aware of all the perks that are potentially available to you as a credit user. While this DOES NOT contain guaranteed shortcuts to getting more money, it will provide you a better understanding of personal credit and how to get the most value out of the money you spend —a key aspect that brings you a step closer to financial independence.

Understanding your credit starts with learning how and why it was formed. The first chapter of this book will introduce you to the early uses of loans, types of credit, and development of credit reporting. Lending and credit reporting aren't as modern as you think.

Contrary to what you may feel about them, credit reports and scores aren't made to make your life difficult. Different entities take these into consideration to measure the risk of dealing with you. As for you, being mindful of your credit history and score can help instill self-discipline. You'll find out how these happen with the help of this book.

Furthermore, you'll learn more about the advantages of having good credit and disadvantages of getting a bad one. Maintaining a favorable credit requires being committed and attentive. Remind yourself of the pros and cons if you get too lazy to fix your credit score.

If you have a bad credit score, you should know that there's still hope. Some lenders may still approve your loan application. However, don't expect them to give you ideal interest rates.

The good news is that you don't have to settle with such deals. With the help of this book, **you'll discover plenty of ways of fixing your credit**. You may apply them first to boost your scores and win better interest rates afterwards. You should know though that repairing your credit can take a lot of time, effort and patience.

On rare occasions, it's hard for some people to get high credit score even if they're doing a lot to improve it and they're handling their finances well. Identity thieves could be blamed for this. **This book will show you how to protect yourself from such criminals.**

Please, leave a review for this book on Amazon

Credit reporting agencies weigh on different factors to determine your FICO scores and VantageScore. Get to know these factors with the help of this book.

The scores aren't as subjective as some people claim. Aside from the factors considered in computing credit scores, **this book will also show you the factors that aren't taken into account.** You have fewer things to worry about if you know precisely which factors don't really affect your credit. That way, you focus your attention on the factors that really matter.

Once you're familiar with the factors, you'll find it easier to correct and control your spending habits. It will also improve the way you set and enforce your budget.

Your credit card use is an important facet of your credit report. Having such card has its pros and cons. In this book, you'll learn about the different types of credit card, along with their respective pros, cons and requirements. Knowing these things will help you choose the right credit card for your needs and get the best rewards.

If you're not that familiar with credit card application, **this book will provide valuable insight into the tiered system that mainly determines what type you can apply for.** This will save you the time and effort of applying for cards that aren't within your reach. In so doing, you'll avoid the penalties that come with rejected credit card applications.

Aside from getting credit cards, this book will teach you how and how not to use them. As you already know, credit card debt is one of the common causes of financial problems for many adults, not just in the US but in other countries.

This book may not *directly* address how to increase your earnings (it might indirectly do so), but it will definitely help you get the most value out of the money you already have.

Do you want to set up a business? This book will show you how to gain access to startup funding. In case you're not aware, getting a loan isn't the only option – there are so many others!

A list of startup funding sources is included in the last portions of this book. Keep on reading to find out how you should get them and why you should.

Without further ado, let's get right into it!

Did You Know?

In 1959, the idea of a "revolving" balance was introduced. This means that cardholders could keep a balance on their credit card without having to pay it off completely every month. While it meant that customers might have to pay finance charges, it also meant that they had more flexibility.

Please, leave a review for this book on Amazon

Chapter 1

History and Evolution of Consumer Credit

Consumer credit makes it easier to pay for goods and services when your funds are low. It might seem like a modern invention, but surprisingly, its earliest forms can be traced back to 3500 BC when Sumerians used consumer loans for agricultural purposes.

In 1800 BC, Babylonians had the Code of Hammurabi. The said code contained the first law covering loans. It stated that annual interest rates should only be around 20% for silver and 33.33% for grains. It also required a contract and a public official as a witness.

Around the 8th century, moral concerns over usury became a subject in Europe. The Church even prohibited the practice. But in 1500, explorations and trade missions boosted the demand for loans.

In 1545, England had a law setting the interest rate at 10%. Two centuries later, Jeremy Bentham presented the treatise "A Defense of Usury". His work detailed the possible disadvantages of limiting interest rates. It also challenged the Church's stand against the practice of making money from loans.

England was also the birthplace for credit reporting. In 1803, local tailors traded information about customers who didn't pay their debts. The Manchester Guardian Society was later established in 1826. The said organization published monthly newsletters about people who didn't settle their debts.

New York caught up with the practice of credit reporting when the Mercantile Agency was created in 1841. It devised a system about the assets and characters of local debtors. It was criticized for being subjective and rumor-based.

When the organization got renamed as R. G. Dun and Company, it used an alphanumeric system for determining credit rating. Such practice was implemented until the 1900s.

In 1899, the Retail Credit Company was established in Atlanta. It would later on become Equifax, one of the biggest credit agencies in the US today.

The practice of using modern-day consumer credit became popular when cars became less expensive but were still not that affordable. General Motors Acceptance Corporation (GMAC) was created in 1919. The Detroit-based corporation provided the first installment-based planning for car purchases. This can be deemed as the oldest form of auto loans.

By 1930, more than 60% of car purchases were done by installment. Appliances and furniture sets became cheaper as well. Installment-based payment also became a practice for buying these products.

Please, leave a review for this book on Amazon

In 1950s, many middle-class Americans already had plenty of credit information. The creation of BankAmericard (now called Visa) further allowed consumers to buy more even when their funds were low. This led to the accumulation of more information about consumers and their debts.

Years later, computer technologies were used to consolidate data. The Fair Credit Reporting Act was also enacted in the country in 1970s. Equifax, Experian and TransUnion have been the biggest enforcers of such act since 1980s. These credit reporting agencies make use of FICO score and VantageScore in providing information about each consumer.

The Need for a Credit Rating System

These days, it's normal to rely on loans to buy homes, cars, appliances and even groceries. But too much dependence leads to financial troubles for irresponsible consumers. This can also cause problems to the lenders.

That's why the need for a universal credit rating system arose. Credit reporting agencies were established to fill this need.

The main aim of credit reporting agencies is to **understand the risks of accepting loan applications from a certain consumer**. When a consumer has bad credit rating, lenders can take it as a proof to deny loan applications. Some lenders may accept such consumer but they tend to manage the risk by increasing the interest rate.

Somehow, credit reports help consumers become more responsible in paying their debts. After all, a good credit rating makes it easier for them to get loans, apply for credit cards, buy homes and even rent properties.

Types of Consumer Credit

Modern-day consumer credit can be categorized into three: installment, revolving and collections. Also dubbed as consumer debt or consumer loan, this lets consumers borrow money for various goods and services, and repay them for different periods.

Installment

The installment type refers to the way you can manage your debt. Auto loans are the most popular type of this consumer credit. These can also be observed when getting appliances and even Heating, Ventilation and Air Conditioning (HVAC) systems. These loans allow you to buy a vehicle even when you can only give 10% downpayment. After giving the downpayment, you'll be required to pay monthly or quarterly fees to cover the capital and interest rates of your loans.

Please, leave a review for this book on Amazon

Mortgages are a lot similar to car loans. But as homes are deemed as assets, loans defaulting on your home or any other real estate property aren't considered as consumer credit. More often than not, products that are purchasable through installment-based consumer credit tend to depreciate after some time. These offerings include groceries, appliances, furniture, clothes, shoes and cars.

There are two ways to get this type of consumer credit. You may apply directly from the establishment or company you're buying from. Another option is to apply for loan from a third-party lending institution or individual.

Revolving

The use of credit card is the most well-known type of revolving consumer credit. It's regarded as revolving because you can keep reusing the card to borrow money and pay for goods and services. With a credit card, consumers can easily purchase different products and services. Unlike the installment type, you'll only need to apply for revolving credit once.

There's a monthly limit on how much credit you can use. This prevents you from excessive use of loans. The limit is mostly dependent on how much you can earn per month. Credit card companies will weigh on your credit rating as well.

Collections

Collections are the final resort when you're unable to pay your debts. Your lenders will seek collection services to ensure that you'll settle your debts whenever you have money. Such services may also get your properties like cars, appliances and furniture especially if you use these as collateral.

The use of consumer credit has its pros and cons. So long as you have self-control, you can be assured that you won't incur too much debt that you can't handle. The rest of this book should equip you with all you need to know in order to make the most out of credit.

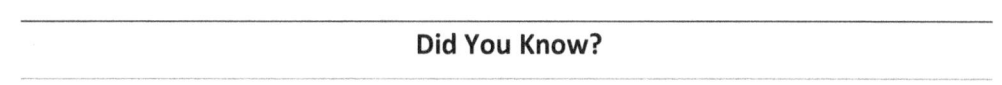

Did You Know?

Closing a credit card account in full will have a negative effect on your credit score. Length of history on an account is 15% of your FICO score.

Please, leave a review for this book on Amazon

Chapter 2

How to Read, Review and Understand Your Credit Report

If you're applying for a housing loan, trying to get a new credit card or simply curious to know your credit standing, you can send an inquiry and request for a copy of your credit report. But even if you are able to get a hold of one, do you know how to read and understand it?

Your credit report contains a lot of information and it may get difficult to navigate. This chapter will enable you to better understand the report:

What is a credit report, exactly?

A credit report is a compilation of valuable information about you and your finances. It paints a picture of how you handle your credit and debt accounts. It shows how much you owe and how you pay them. It looks at both your current and historical financial status.

In the U.S. there are three credit bureaus or credit reporting agencies that maintain your credit information. They are Equifax, Experian and Trans Union. The companies you do business with send updated debt information to these credit bureaus and they then will update the credit report.

The actual credit report contains several sections that tackle various factors that creditors look at when evaluating your credit viability.

Generally, your credit report will have the following information:

Credit Score

The credit score is a number that represents a consumer's credit worthiness. It shows past and current information about a consumer's credit account.

This is a three-digit number that ranges from 300 to 850 that reflects your creditworthiness to lenders. Creditors use this as a decision-making tool in processing credit applications such as loans and credit cards.

The higher the credit score, the lower the risk for lenders. This metric is discussed in detail in the next chapter.

Personal Identifying information

This section of the credit report includes personally identifying information such as your complete name and known aliases, your social security number, date of birth, contact number and previous and current addresses.

It also includes relevant information on employers as well as employment status.

Please, leave a review for this book on Amazon

Credit Account History

This section reflects the history and details of all your credit accounts – both open and closed ones. This is divided into two streams: revolving accounts which includes credit cards, and installment accounts like mortgages or student loads.

Each entry will have the following information: account type, account number, lender, dates opened, credit limit, amount owed and current account status.

Public Record Information

Ideally, this section should be blank. If not, this section will show any open legal issues related to your financial situation. This includes cases of bankruptcy, tax and other liens, judgments and even overdue child support.

These issues have significant negative impact on your credit score.

Inquiries

This section lists the companies that requested your credit report. It would show the inquiry date, the purpose of the inquiry and how long the inquiry will be reflected in your credit report.

Only the following are legally allowed to submit an inquiry:

- Employers,
- Insurance companies,
- Lenders and
- Yourself.

Personal Statement

This section of the report is optional and voluntary. Consumers can make a 100-word statement to dispute presented data, explain your side of the story or alert lenders to an error in dispute. Personal statements do not impact your credit score.

What are the benefits of credit reporting?

Credit reporting is important. No matter where you go, your credit follows you through life. Knowing your credit standing can help you make many decisions about your financial future in many ways.

Your credit report serves as a snapshot of your financial status. It enables you to understand your own financial capacity to commit to credit obligations.

Please, leave a review for this book on Amazon

Businesses, lenders, potential employers and landlords can check your credit report to make decisions about you, especially those that relate to financial gains or losses.

With a credit report, you are updated on your level of creditworthiness, which can help you get approvals and better interest rates on loans.

Finally, regularly checking your credit report can help you protect your identity. **You can tell if someone else is using your identity by simply reading the report**. If there are accounts listed that you did not open, you can file a dispute, and then have your credit report reviewed and corrected.

How can you request for copies of your credit report?

All U.S. citizens are entitled to request and receive a free credit report every 12 months from each of the three nationwide credit report companies.

- Equifax (www.equifax.com)
- Experian (www.experian.com)
- Trans Union (www.transunion.com)

These companies created multiple channels in which you can request for a copy. You can go online and check the central website, call a toll-free hotline number or mail a completed form through a P.O. Box. The details of each option is presented below:

- Website: www.annualcreditreport.com

You need to fill out the online order form and submit. The report should be accessible immediately upon requesting

- Toll-Free Number: 1-877-322-8228

After calling the toll-free number, your request will be processed and mailed to you at your noted return address within 15 days

- Mail

You need to submit a completed Annual Credit Report Request Form and mail to: Annual Credit Report Request Service, P.O. Box 105281, Atlanta, GA 30348-5281

Mail requests will be processed and results will be mailed within 15 days of receipt.

Citizens are allowed to order one free copy of your report from each of the reporting companies every 12 months.

Please, leave a review for this book on Amazon

Upon requesting, you will need to give your complete legal name, social security number, address and date of birth. Credit reporting companies may request for other information that only you would know, like your loan repayment structure, to validate your identity.

What if there are inaccuracies or incomplete information in your credit report?

If you find errors, inaccuracies or incomplete information in your credit report, you can easily file a dispute with the credit bureau. There are several ways to file a dispute:

- Online dispute through the credit bureau's website:
    - Equifax Disputes: (https://www.equifax.com/personal/disputes/)
    - Experian Disputes: (https://www.experian.com/disputes)
    - Transunion Disputes: (http://www.disputes.transunion.com)

- Send a letter via certified mail to the credit bureau. In your letter, identify what you believe needs to be corrected. Attach a copy of your credit report and highlight the items in question. Include copies of documents that support your claim as well.

As of the moment though, only Trans Union receives dispute via mail. Both Equifax and Experian process all dispute via the online channel.

Send mail to:

TransUnion LLC

Consumer Dispute Center

P.O.Box 2000

Chester, PA 19016

The credit reporting company must investigate the items in question within 30 days upon receipt of dispute. After the investigation is completed and the report is found inaccurate, the company will make the necessary adjustments and notify all credit reporting companies. They must also give you written investigation results and a free copy of the corrected report.

The information in your credit report significantly impacts your life. It is, then, important to ensure that the information declared in that report is accurate and updated. Make it a habit to regularly request for your credit report. Checking every 6- months or once a year should be sufficient.

Please, leave a review for this book on Amazon

However, if you suspect that someone else is using your identity, then it is best to conduct these checks more frequently.

See the box below for a sample mail you can send to the bureau if you're looking to file for a dispute.

10 November 2018

John H. Smith

1234 Broad Street, New York, NY 10024

Complaint Department

TransUnion LLC

Consumer Dispute Center, P.O.Box 2000

Chester, PA 19016

Dear Sir or Madam:

I recently obtained a copy of my credit report from your agency and found the following item to be in error:

I dispute [VISA credit card] account number [4000 1234 5678 9000]. This account has been paid in full as of September 15, 2018.

I am requesting that the item be updated to correct the information. I've attached copies of the bank statements reflecting the payments I made and supporting my position on this claim. Please investigate this matter and correct the dispute claim as soon as possible.

Sincerely,

John Smith

Enclosures: VISA 4000 1234 5678 9000 September Statement

Chapter 3

Understanding Your Credit Score

Your credit score is a powerful number that impacts your present life and your future in a multitude of ways. It is a three-digit number that represents your creditworthiness to lenders. It serves as their guide in approving or disapproving your loan or credit card applications. It also determines the interest rates that will be applied to your mortgages, auto loans and cash loans.

This figure is calculated based on your available credit information. This score is then evaluated by lenders to determine your credibility as a borrower.

A credit score can change from time to time. These changes occur depending on a consumer's financial behavior including when paying a loan. It also takes into account whether the consumer can manage to pay the loan in the long term.

Understanding your credit score helps you determine whether you are keeping your credit healthy. It can also help you keep your credit score in check.

In the US, credit scores are developed using scoring models such as FICO and VantageScore. This section will focus on FICO in particular although VantageScore has its dedicated chapter. This is to provide you a broader view of what's involved in generating credit scores.

The FICO Score

The FICO credit score is the prevailing credit scoring system. It is developed by FICO, a company that specializes in predictive analytics. With this system, they look at a set of credit information to create scores and forecast a consumer's behavior using the same parameters.

FICO Scores gives an accurate prediction of how well a consumer will be able to handle their loans including how they could pay their loans on time and their ability to manage their credit given a higher credit line.

How FICO Scores are Calculated

FICO Scores are calculated based on the following factors. This is just an overview of how the scoring model arrives at your score. These factors will be discussed in detail in Chapter 7.

- Payment history comprises 35% of your score. This reflects how responsible you are with your payments.

- Your total debts make up 30% of the score.

- The duration of your credit history comprises 15%.

- 10% is allocated to current or new credit inquiries.

Please, leave a review for this book on Amazon

- The last 10% goes to the diversity of your credit accounts.

Other score models also use the same factors. Therefore, a good FICO score indicates that that you are likely to also get a good score on other credit score standards.

What's a Good FICO Score?

Anything that's at least 670 is considered a good FICO rating. Nonetheless, you should still aim for a higher score because it can give you better interests when applying for loans and discounts when buying real estate, among other benefits as will be discussed in a short while.

The FICO Score Range

Your FICO score can fall between 300 and 850 with the lower number representing more risk for the lender. A good credit score makes it possible to buy your dream home, your own luxury vehicle or open a business. A bad score, usually less than 500, may present challenges in attaining the same things.

- ❖ **Poor (300-559)**

Scores that fall within this range are way under the standard score. If you're in this range, it shows lenders that giving you a loan is risky. You probably won't be able to get loan applications approved except perhaps when there's collateral.

- ❖ **Fair (580 – 669)**

This is the gray zone. It's still under the standard score of consumers but you still won't get great credit deals. If you're in this range, some lenders may approve loan requests. In fact, some of them will still consider this a poor score. However, you may still get subprime loans especially if there are extenuating circumstances

- ❖ **Good (670 - 739)**

Many consumers have a credit score that falls within this range. Most lenders will see this as an acceptable score because it's not risky. Only about 8% of applicants with a score that fall within this range are likely to become seriously delinquent.

- ❖ **Very Good (740-799)**

This score is higher than the standard score of consumers. If your score is in this range, lenders can see that you are a responsible consumer and you'll be getting good interest rates.

- ❖ **Excellent 800-850**

This score is way higher than the standard score of consumers. In this range the lenders see that you are an excellent consumer.

The FICO Score Range was recently updated to FICO Score 9, but most lenders still use the old FICO score range.

The Importance of a Good Credit Score

There are many ways in which a good credit score can benefit you as a consumer.

1. Higher chances of loan approval

A good credit score increases your chances of getting your loan applications approved, and the process will be faster too. A good credit score tells lenders that you are diligent in paying your dues. This indicates that you are not a risky 'investment' and this attracts lenders to do business with you.

2. Getting the best credit card deals

Banks will likely approve your credit card application because a good score reassures banks that you can handle your credit and pay your bills on time.

3. Lower interest rates.

Interest costs money so having good credit that helps you get the lowest interest rate possible saves a lot of money in the long run. And since lenders will see you as a reliable investment, you are likely to get the best structured loans.

4. Higher credit limits

The increase in credit limit due to good credit scores will not only allow you more access to credit. It will also improve your credit utilization ratio, which means even better credit scores. Just be careful about requesting for a higher credit limits though because it usually means that the issuer will perform a hard inquiry, which will factor into your credit score.

5. More bargaining power

A good credit score allow you to negotiate for the best loan structures. This is because banks and lenders see you as a guaranteed business and asset that can return in the future.

6. Better car insurance premiums

Many states ban the practice of car insurance providers using credit scores to assess insurance premiums. However, in states where it is allowed, most insurers will check your score and reward those with higher scores because they believe that those who have good credit are predisposed to behavior that reduces risk.

7. Better Rates for Mortgage Loans

When you're buying something as high-priced as real estate, a small difference in interest rates, say between% 4 and 4.25%, can add up.

Please, leave a review for this book on Amazon

8. Getting Rental Approvals

Renting an apartment will be easier with a good credit score. Landlords look at your credit score to see if you can assure on-time payments on rent.

9. Less Security Deposits

You will be asked to pay less deposit or none at all when acquiring a new apartment or phone. This is because a good credit score indicates that you are a low-risk tenant/customer and will be likely to pay your bills on time.

10. Better quality of life

This is the best reason why you want a good credit score. You don't have to worry about your landlord coming to evict you from your home. You would want to get your loan applications approved if you need to build that dream house. A life with less stress can make you happier than most.

Downside of having a low credit score

A good credit score will help you in the long term because you can get prime deals with lenders and banks. A low credit score on the hand can become a nightmare and will cause you so much stress and difficulties in the long run.

1. Having your loans declined

Lenders and banks will likely decline loans made with a low credit score. This is due to the risky nature of lending your money.

2. High Interest Rates

Low credit scores show the probability of a consumer of being delinquent. A lender or bank might let such an individual to borrow from them with the caveat that the interest rates are higher and the credit line is smaller. After all, they will be cautious in lending your money.

3. Declined credit card applications and low credit limit

Credit card companies usually look for consumers who can use their cards well. Delinquent payments and going over the credit limit are a no-no. These practices can lead to low credit scores, which in turn, increase the probability of having your credit card application declined.

Even if you get a credit card application approved, it will still have a low credit limit. Banks will be wary of giving you a higher credit limit for fear of you not paying your dues.

4. High deposits and difficulty in renting apartments

Landlords may check an individual's credit score to determine if he should charge a deposit. This is especially true for well-established landlords in prime lots and areas. If you have a poor credit score which indicates that you are more likely to be unable to pay rent, he may require an even bigger security deposit to compensate for the risk. You may have to end up renting a place in in less desirable areas.

5. Setting up a small business will be a challenge

You'll probably need a loan from the bank in putting up a business. Banks are likely to be reluctant to lend start-up money to those with low credit score. What they like to see is your ability to pay on time.

6. Finding a job can be a challenge

Some companies take your credit score into consideration when running a background check because of the nature of the job. Potential employees who are going to work for financial institutions are also asked about their credit scores. This is because some employees believe that credit scores indicate whether or not someone is able to handle responsibilities.

7. Higher Insurance Premiums

Low credit score can play a part in getting home or car insurance with higher premium. Insurance companies experience more claims from clients with lower credit scores than most. They fear people who have low credit score to file fraudulent claims.

8. Difficulty in getting a new car

Getting a new car with a low credit score will also be difficult. Car companies can decline your car loan when they see that your credit history indicates poor credit. This is indicated by delinquent payments on your car loan and repossession.

9. Difficulty buying a house.

Banks and lenders check a consumer's ability to pay for their home loans. Foreclosures, repossessions, and delayed payments in your history will decrease your chances of getting a home loan.

10. Calls from debt collectors

A life spent hounded by the constant ringing of the phone is not ideal. But it may become norm if you have bad credit, as banks and lenders will ask collectors to go after you.

Please, leave a review for this book on Amazon

What to do if you have no FICO Score

At the start, you may not have credit yet. But building your credit score may not be as hard as you think.

The first option is to become an authorized user on someone else's credit card. This is likely going to be your parents. You can set up an agreement with your parent on how you can pay for your purchases. Remember that you won't be legally obligated to pay for them but if the primary shareholder expects you to pay your share, then do so. Ask the card issuer if they report authorized user activity.

You can also ask other people to co-sign a loan or credit card line. This will in turn help you understand the responsibilities of having credit. Co-signing with them requires you to pay half of the dues.

You may also apply for loan for credit-building. This loan has the sole purpose of building credit, which makes it perfect for those who have little to no history. It works like a savings account in which you will not really "borrow" money in the strictest sense of the word. You will be periodically paying an amount and your payments will be reported to the credit bureaus. You can then collect the money after the "loan" is repaid. You can start your search online. Credit unions and community banks are the ones that usually offer these. It might take a while to find one because they're not widely advertised.

Fourth, you can build credit through secured credit cards. Secured credit cards require you to have an initial deposit equal to your credit limit. They are used for a limited time.

Finally, you can build credit through rent. Ask your landlord if he reports your rent to authorized rent trackers. Some scoring models do not include this in their calculation, but then some lenders do consider them.

How to achieve a 700+ credit score

It is possible to achieve a 700+ credit score if you do the following:

1. Build good credit right at the start.

Pay your dues on time and pay them in full. It will definitely help in increasing your credit score. Take into account that the FICO Score puts heavy weight on this.

2. Use your credit well.

Do not go over your credit limit. It is wise to use as little of your credit as possible. This will show that you have good control in money expenditure.

Please, leave a review for this book on Amazon

3. Avoid getting hard inquiries.

Note that hard inquiries lower your score. Soft inquiries are fine. To manage this, only apply for a new credit account if you absolutely need it.

4. Use various credit accounts.

It is a good idea to have various credit accounts provided you are able to handle them well. Additionally, mixed accounts can also be a benefit. It will show how well you are able to manage different types of accounts and still be able to pay for them all.

5. Avoid closing accounts too soon.

Having various accounts can be beneficial if you manage them well. It is better to close them if you don't. But be careful because the duration of the account also factor into your score. Also, make sure you don't close several accounts all at the same time. This may hurt your credit score. Don't remove your oldest account because it will contribute to your credit history.

6. Avoid having negative marks.

Negative credit information can lower your credit scores. Foreclosures, repossessions and a history of delayed payments are negative marks. Review and check your credit score from time to time. Make sure to report any error in your credit history to avoid the lowering of your credit score.

As we go through the next few chapters, you will learn more about how your financial behavior can affect your credit scores and what you can do to maintain healthy credit. For now, remember that consistency is the key. Be diligent and handle your credits well. In time your credit score will increase and reach a score of 700.

Did Your Know?

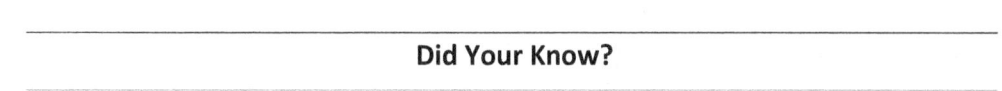

Mastercard began life as MasterCharge and was formed by four Californian banks in 1967. It became Mastercard in 1979 and it was the first card to use holograms.

Please, leave a review for this book on Amazon

Chapter 4

Monitoring Credit Reports and Credit Scores

Credit monitoring safeguards consumers from possible fraud. They secure accounts from identity theft issues and suspicious activities.

What are credit-monitoring services?

Credit monitoring services allow consumers to track their credit report and credit score. Through this type of service, consumers are notified of any changes in their accounts. The notice comes in the form of e-mails or text alerts.

Among the activities that automatically alert consumers are as follows:

- New account openings (e.g., credit cards and loans)
- New credit inquiries
- New public records (i.e., information on bankruptcies, court judgments)
- Changes in home address
- Late payments and/or unpaid debts

How to check your credit score

There are many ways to find out a credit score. It can be checked by the consumer manually. It can also be determined with the help of agencies or through various online resources.

For the manual procedure, a consumer may look through his financial statements. These may be from credit cards, financial institutions, or loan statements. Consumers can also opt to log in to their online accounts to check their credit score.

Consumers can also use credit score services from sites. This, however, may come at a price. Some credit scoring sites offer credit scores for free. While others require their customers to pay monthly subscription fee.

Consumers are not limited to these options. They can also check their credit score from agencies or from specific online sites. Among the agencies that provide this kind of service are Equifax, Experian, and TransUnion. These agencies use credit scoring models to determine a consumer's credit score. They also make use of various data to calculate credit scores.

If you're from the US, you can also go to www.annualcreditreport.com to check your credit scores. The site provides a copy of credit report from major credit bureaus. Consumers can get a copy of their credit scores at least once in every 12 months. Revisit the previous chapter to get more information on how to get your credit score

Hard and Soft Credit Inquiries

Hard Inquiry occurs when a prospective lender looks into a consumer's credit report. This type of inquiry helps a lender determine whether the consumer qualifies for a loan. It happens when a consumer applies for a credit card, car loan, or mortgage.

On the other hand, a Soft Inquiry is when a person or company does a background check on a consumer's credit report. Soft Inquiry is done so that a lender can determine whether the consumer is still creditworthy. The lender checks for signs of risk on lending matters. Soft Inquiry can be done without the consumer's permission.

These types of credit inquiries both check one's credit score. They only differ on the impact they have on the credit score itself.

While Soft Inquiry does not have any effect on a credit, Hard Inquiry does. Hard Inquiry slightly lowers credit scores. It also remains on a consumer's account record for two years. This is what consumers should be concerned about.

Numerous hard inquiries could indicate two things. One, a consumer may be desperate for credit. Or two, he did not succeed in borrowing from previous creditors for whatever reason.

Because of these, it would be best for consumers to maintain low records of hard inquiries. Large volumes of hard inquiries mean high level of risk. As a result, lenders become wary of potential clients with numerous records. Worse, lenders might reject them since they are perceived to be more likely to file for bankruptcy in the future.

Types of monitoring services available

It is important to maintain a healthy credit report and score since they determine a consumer's creditworthiness. Credit monitoring services help consumers check their credit reports and scores.

There are numerous credit monitoring firms offering services to consumers. The three major credit bureaus (Equifax, Experian, and TransUnion) also provide monitoring services. Other monitoring services can be accessed online through www.annualcreditreport.com.

Some of the best monitoring services available are Identity Guard, Credit Karma, and Identity Force.

Identity Guard provides protection against identity theft. It has a mobile app that notifies consumers of changes in their credit records. It allows consumers to check their credit reports monthly from the three major credit bureaus. Identity Guard also comes with a million dollars' worth of insurance against identity theft.

Please, leave a review for this book on Amazon

Credit Karma, on the other hand, offers free monitoring services. It allows consumers access to credit reports at any time. Compared to Identity Guard, Credit Karma provides consumers access to only two of the major credit bureaus – TransUnion and Equifax. Here, credit report is updated weekly.

Identity Force is the monitoring service with the most security features. In addition to identity monitoring and credit monitoring services, Identity Force also monitors consumer's personal information. It also notifies consumers whether their accounts have been compromised. It also comes with an insurance policy worth $1 million.

Credit information services such as monitoring, credit scoring, or applications that oversee accounts, may come at a hefty price. However, they're crucial in this day and age where there is so much data mining that occur all over the world.

Did You Know?

It is against the merchant agreements of Mastercard, Visa, and American Express for a vendor to require you to provide your phone number, home address or other personal information. You also do not need to present a driver's license or spend above a certain purchase amount.

Please Kindly Review This Book

If you have found any value from reading this book, please kindly post a review letting us know about it. It'll only take a minute of your time. Thank you so much!

Please, leave a review for this book on Amazon

Chapter 5

The VantageScore Model

Equifax, Experian and TransUnion collaborated to develop and introduce a new credit score model that can compete with the FICO model - the VantageScore. The process for FICO and VantageScore are almost the same but with a slight difference on the outcome of the credit scores.

What is a good VantageScore?

In VantageScore 3.0's scoring model, scores range from 300-850. A rating of 700 and above is considered good, while a rating of 750 and above is considered excellent.

However, VantageScore 4.0 is going to be released very soon.

VantageScore Ranges Explained

A credit score of 300-549 is rated as very poor and applicants with this number are unlikely to be extended credit.

550-649 credit score is rated as poor and applicants in this range could be extended some credit but they may experience certain conditions such as larger down payments.

A credit rating between 650 and 699 is rated as Fair that allows an applicant for credit but they are unlikely to get a competitive rate.

A score of 700-749 is good. Credit applications from people with this rating are accepted and come at competitive rates.

Lastly, a credit score of 750-850 is rated as excellent and applicants with these scores get the best and most competitive rates on credit accounts.

How VantageScore calculates your credit score

VantageScore categorizes credit information into six. These categories have different levels of influence on your credit scores. Here is how VantageScore groups the importance of credit score data:

- Payment history: extreme influence

- Age and type of credit: high influence

- Percentage of used credit limit: high influence

- Total balances and debt: moderate influence

- Recent credit behavior and inquiries: less influence

Please, leave a review for this book on Amazon

- Available credit: less influence

Differences between the FICO and VantageScore Models

FICO and VantageScore are the most known credit-scoring models offered by different Credit Reporting Agencies. The process for FICO and VantageScore are almost the same but there are some differences in rules and processes.

1. Length of Credit History required

In order to get a FICO score, the consumer must already have an existing one or more credit accounts that have already been reported to the rightful credit-scoring agency. It must have been open for the last six months and been reported within the last six months.

VantageScore, on the other hand, allows applications from consumers with one month of credit history so long as it is an account reported within the last two years.

Because of this, VantageScore can provide information to consumers who did not qualify with FICO, thereby offering convenience.

2. Significance of Late Payments

Your late payments matter both to your FICO and VantageScore accounts. They both look into these records:

- When did your last late payment occur?
- In how many of your accounts did late payments occur?
- How many payments on an account have you missed?

Late payments have an impact on your credit score, but the difference between these models is that, FICO penalizes these late payments equally. While in VantageScore, late payments for mortgages give a huge disadvantage to consumers. So if you've been having problems with your mortgage, you might have a better FICO score than in VantageScore.

3. Impact of Credit Inquiries

Deduplications happen when a consumer inquires for credit loans in which lenders send the application to other lenders, causing your account to reflect multiple inquiries. The difference is that FICO uses a 45-day span to deduplicate your inquiries while VantageScore only gives a 14-day span. Be wary of credit inquiry especially when you are planning for a house or car loan because it might become a "hard inquiry" that can lower your credit score.

Please, leave a review for this book on Amazon

4. Effect of Low-Balance Collections

When your account is given to a collection agency, FICO ignores all the collections that have a balance lower than $100. As for VantageScore, it ignores the collections regardless of the original balance of the account.

Chapter 6

Factors That Impact Your Credit Rating

Improving your credit score requires understanding the factors that impact your score. Having this information will help you make informed financial decisions that will impact your score. Remember, the higher your credit score, the better the chance of getting the credit you need.

Note that FICO and VantageScore have fundamentally different methodologies in coming up with your credit score. FICO, however, is the more ubiquitous which is why their system was used as basis for this chapter.

Nonetheless, here's a chart that should give a quick overview of the similarities and differences of the two

Fico Score Weights	Vantage Score Weights
Payment History 35%	Payment History 40%
Credit Utilization 30%	Credit Utilization 20%
Age of Credit Accounts 15%	Age and Diversity of Credit accounts 21%
Credit Diversity 10%	Total Balances/Debt 11%
New Credit 10%	New Credit and Available Credit 8%

But essentially, there are five key factors that impact your credit score. They are payment history, credit utilization, the age of accounts, credit diversity and recent credit history. Together these factors define the characteristics of the borrower. It estimates the chance of default and assess the risk of a potential financial loss to the lender.

Payment History

Credit Score Weight: 35%

Payment history is the most important factor in calculating your credit score. This usually makes up a good part of your score. It is a measure of your ability to settle your bills on schedule.

Your past long-term paying trend is used to forecast future long-term behavior. Generally, missing your due date for a couple of days isn't so bad. Still, you should make it a habit to pay bills on time. Note that you may be charged late payment fees or reconnection fees to have services back. And that's not the only bad thing that comes with late payment.

Your credit score will be affected when companies report a late payment incident to the credit bureau. FICO, for example, will note this incident and consider other factors to determine how your action will impact your score.

They will be looking at your most recent reported missed due date incident, review the frequency of late payments in the past and aggregate the amount owed from all your credit accounts.

Serious payment related issues such as irregular payments, collections, repossessions, or a foreclosure can destroy your credit score and make it extremely difficult to get approved for anything that would require good credit.

To improve your credit score:

Make sure that you make all your bill payments on time each month. To do this, you can set-up payment reminders in your calendar, revise payment due date to align with your paycheck or enroll your accounts to an auto-pay service. These actions will automate the manual task of remembering to settle your bills on time.

If you have a tendency to forget or struggle to make payments on time, consider setting your accounts for automatic payments.

You can request to change your bill due dates to better align with your paycheck.

Credit Utilization

Credit Score Weight: 30%

Credit utilization is the ratio of your balance to the total credit available. To simplify, it is the amount of the credit that you are actually using.

Note that FICO looks at credit utilization in two parts. First, you'll get a separate credit utilization score for each of your credit cards. Then, your total credit utilization will be calculated in which your total balance is compared to your total credit limit. If you get a bad score in any of the two categories, your credit score could be damaged. This means that you should keep an eye not just on one account but all of them. Even if you handled a few of them really well but overlooked one or two, you could be in for a poor score.

Please, leave a review for this book on Amazon

To get a good credit utilization score, you should maintain low credit card balances. Those who habitually max out credit cards or almost always reach their credit limit tend to be viewed as a potentially irresponsible debtor and therefore a risk.

With credit utilization, the guideline is "the lower, the better." Having high balances will heavily impact your credit score. So to keep within acceptable limits, try not to go over 30% of your available credit. To illustrate, if you have $1,000 credit card limit, you should use no more than $300 monthly. Apply this 30% guideline to the total combined limit of all your available credit.

To improve this aspect of your credit score:

The simplest way is to manage your spending habits. Be careful when requesting a credit limit increase in your existing accounts because it's a hard inquiry and can therefore lower your credit score. Make early payments throughout your billing cycle if you are not able to do the first two options.

Age of Accounts

Credit Score Weight: 15%

This refers to the average age of your credit accounts. To measure this, lenders take into account three things: the average age of all accounts from open date to the present, the age of the earliest opened account and the age of the most recently opened account. To compute the average age of your accounts, scoring models sum up the months of all the accounts in your credit report (this is from the open date to the present) and then divide the total by the number of accounts.

A long-established credit history provides a clearer snapshot of your long-term financial behavior. So, as a principle: "the lengthier your credit history, the better the score." But those that don't have long histories can still garner great credit scores if they have consistent on-time payments and have low utilization ratios.

To improve your credit score:

Raise the average age of your accounts by avoiding the practice of constantly opening new accounts. Only do it if you absolutely have to. But if you already have new ones, let them age; don't close them just yet.

Leave your oldest accounts open and active. This will show your ability to manage credit over time.

Think carefully before canceling your cards or closing credit accounts especially those that you've had for some time. Long standing accounts can positively influence your credit score.

Please, leave a review for this book on Amazon

Credit Mix

Credit Score Weight: 10%

Creditors prefer consumers that maintain a diverse credit mix. People who hold different types of credit accounts can get a high credit score. Having varied accounts show that you are able to effectively manage multiple types of loans.

Credit accounts include installment loans and revolving credit. Installment loans such as student loans, auto loans, home equity loans, signature loans, credit builder loans and mortgages usually involve a fixed monthly payment and a scheduled repayment structure.

Revolving credit accounts include credit cards and home equity lines of credit. With this type of credit, there's usually a set limit that you can borrow from regularly. People with no credit cards tend to be viewed as higher risk compared to those that are able to manage their cards responsibly.

To improve your credit score:

Consider getting installment loans. A personal installment loan may be helpful. You may also opt for a low-rate auto loan and then just pay it off as soon as possible. Even if you pay it in just a few months, it would still count as an installment loan.

Try not to do business with finance companies. Their rates and terms are not as good as those from banks and credit unions.

Get a credit card. Keep a low or even no balance. If you have poor or no credit score, you can still get a secured credit card.

Apply for and open new credit accounts only as needed.

Recent Credit History

Credit Score Weight: 10%

New or recent credit is important because it can make you seem like a risky investment to lenders.

Here are the factors that are considered under this category.

- The accounts you've opened in the last 6 to 12 months
- The ratio of new accounts to old ones
- The number of credit inquiries particularly hard inquiries and how long it's been since the last one

- How long it has been since you opened the newest account
- The reappearance of positive credit information for an account that used to reflect payment problems

To improve your credit score:

Open a new account or two but do not overdo it. Remember that if you open too many accounts, the hard inquiries will show up on your report and damage your score. Only consider what you need and apply for a loan when the time is right. Be patient and build your credit score over time.

It is good to note that inquiries completely disappear from your credit report after 24 months. Only inquiries made in the last 12 months factor into your credit score. So, try to review your credit rating periodically and keep yourself updated.

Avoid regularly opening new credit accounts.

Open new credit accounts with long intervals between each application. Avoid opening multiple accounts over a short period of time.

The Bottomline

These factors are considered in all credit score models. Knowing the weights placed on each factor will give you a better idea on where to focus your attention.

In this case, with a total of 65% weight in computing for your credit score, credit history and credit utilization are the needle movers. This basically means that you need to do these three things right now to help manage your credit score. These are things that you have direct control over and can easily handle.

Lastly, remember that it is important to check your own credit report regularly. It is a smart move especially if you aim to keep a healthy credit score. These personal and soft inquiries don't cost a thing and don't affect your credit rating. It also gives you a better view of your financial standing real-time.

Did You Know?

A common clause in the terms and conditions is that the cardholder waives their right to sue the credit card company.

Please, leave a review for this book on Amazon

Chapter 7

Factors That Do Not Affect Your Credit Score

Those who are worrying that their credit scores are affected by every financial decision they make may be in for a surprise. Here are some factors that do not affect your credit scores.

Income

Your credit reports do record your employment history but it doesn't affect your credit scores, neither does your current income. Keep in mind, though, that your income may have an effect on how you are paying your bills, because this one does impact your credit scores.

If you have applied for a loan before, you'll remember that you were asked to provide information regarding the amount of your monthly income through your employment certificate and copies of your pay slips and income tax returns. These only influence the maximum amount of loan you can get but not your credit scores.

Age

Age does not impact your credit scores although the credit reports do record your day of birth. However, 15% of your total credit score is related to the age of the accounts you have at the moment.

Marital Status

Credit reports record your marriage status as well as the name of your spouse but neither affect credit scores. Your credit scores also don't merge or link with your spouse's when you tie the knot. Each of you will have separate credit scores and reports.

Education

Whether you graduate from Harvard or from some online education system, it won't be recorded in the credit reports. Neither will the degree program you completed. But some lenders may consider your educational attainment and the employment which you acquired through your background. This might be part of their application process.

Location

Your credit reports have your place of residence but it won't be used in scoring your credit. Your location might have impact on your insurance rates as well as property taxes but not on your credit standing.

Criminal Record

If you go to jail, your credit reports will have a notation of the event but your credit scores remain the same. However, some other factors arising from you being getting some jail time might significantly affect your credit standing. These include civil judgments like overdue child support, tax liens, monetary judgments due to collection accounts, and bankruptcy. Also, court costs and fines that you are not able to settle on time and sent to collections will appear on the reports.

Net Worth

Just like your income, the amount of assets under your name can help you get a bigger loan amount but if you already have a bad credit score, you won't get approved. However, liens you have on your house like mortgage will appear on credit reports.

Debit Cards

Debit card activities don't get reported to credit agencies so you won't get to build credit if you keep using debit cards on your favorite restaurants and stores. The same applies to cash and checks. Your credit card is the only plastic that impacts your credit score.

Gender and Religion

These are some types of information that you need to put in when applying for loans and credit cards and they are recorded in your credit reports but whether you're a male or female, Christian or Muslim, does not impact your credit scores.

Did You Know?

There is an online dating service called CreditScoreDating.com for those who are concerned with the financial situation of a potential mate. The site's motto is "Credit Scores Are Sexy".

Please, leave a review for this book on Amazon

Chapter 8

Credit Cards

So What Exactly Is A Credit Card? A credit card is a type of payment card. It is issued to allow users or cardholders to pay for goods and services without the use of cash. The amount that you can spend is based on the credit card agreement that you have signed. In the future, you are obliged to pay the agreed amount and the charges that come with it.

How Credit Cards Work (Consumer Side)

The card issuer, which is usually a bank, grants a line of credit to you and creates a revolving account. MasterCard and Visa are some of the most popular payment processors for credit cards. The issuing bank provides the necessary paperwork for the user or soon-to-be card holder before he or she can acquire a payment card.

The revolving account represents the debts of the borrower. The outstanding balance or the unpaid, interest-bearing balance of a loan portfolio doesn't have to be paid fully every month.

However, every month, the credit card holder may be required to pay a specific minimum amount based on the amount of money owed to the lender or bank. Nevertheless, the user can pay the issuer any amount between the full balance and the minimum payment.

If he or she can't deposit the minimum payment required at the end of the monthly billing period, the remaining monthly balance will roll over into the following month.

In this case, the issuer will charge the holder with an interest that is based on the required monthly minimum payment. The interest will be added to the remaining balance.

How Credit Cards Work (Business Side)

A card issuer, such as a credit union or a bank, enters into a deal or an agreement with merchants so that they will accept their payment cards. Merchants advertise the type of cards they accept. They display acceptance marks.

With respect to credit cards, an acceptance mark is a design or logo that indicates the card schemes that a merchant or ATM accepts. In restaurants, this is particularly indicated at the bottom of the menu.

Please, leave a review for this book on Amazon

The issuer provides the card to the customer after or during the time that the credit provider approves the account of the borrower. The provider need not be the same business entity as the issuer.

After receiving the card, the user can utilize it to pay for certain goods and services. The user consents to pay by entering his or her PIN or by signing a receipt. The receipt contains the details of the card and indicates the amount that has to be paid.

Nowadays, many merchants accept verbal authorizations (i.e. electronic) by means of the internet or through a telephone. Electronic authorization is also known as CNP or Card Not Present Transaction.

A CNP, Mail Order or Telephone Order is a transaction made in which the cardholder can't present the card for a seller's visual examination. Electronic verification systems enable merchants to validate whether the presented card is valid or not and to verify whether or not the cardholder has enough credits for the requested service or item.

The verification or transaction is performed using a point-of-sale, or a credit card payment terminal. The card's data, such as the name of the user and the available credits, is obtained from a chip or a magnetic stripe on the card.

For CNP transactions, in which the card can't be physically presented or confirmed, merchants will also validate that the client owns the card. They do this by asking for the security code, the customer's billing address, and the card's date of expiry. The security code is printed at the back of the card.

Credit Card Versus Line of Credit

A revolving account represents the actual debt and its generated interest every payment period, whereas, a line of credit or LOC is a credit source that is extended to a business, individual, or government by a financial institution. There are many forms of line of credit. It can come in the form of overdraft line of credit, traditional revolving credit card account, and term loans.

In other words, an LOC can be a source of funds. It is an arrangement between a customer and a financial institution. It establishes the maximum amount that the client can borrow. He or she can access funds from the LOC anytime.

However, the borrower can't spend or withdraw more than the maximum amount set. This can also happen when the borrower fails to meet requirements like timely payments.

Please, leave a review for this book on Amazon

Cash Advances

Generally, a credit card allows the holder to borrow money as a cash advance or as payment to a merchant or entity. A cash advance is a short-term loan from a financial institution such as a bank or any alternative lender. Most credit card issuers provide this service.

With a cash advance, the cardholder can withdraw cash either over the counter or through ATM. Cash advances incur a fee of more or less 5% of the debt. Often, the interest is higher than other forms of credit card transactions.

Depending on the guidelines included in the agreement, there are specific purchases made using a credit card which are considered to be cash advances. Examples are prepaid debit cards, lottery tickets, gaming chips, and certain fees and taxes paid to the government. Such transactions also have a high-interest rate and don't have a grace period.

There are times when merchants fail to disclose the actual nature of a transaction. In this case, the deal is processed as a standard credit card transaction.

Often, merchants pass the processing fees on to the cardholders despite the guidelines. In some agreements, it is indicated that users must not incur extra fees for paying using a credit card.

Billing and Payment

Every month, the user receives a statement that indicates the total amount owed, any outstanding fees, and the transactions made using the card. The cardholder must pay a specified minimum amount every month in order to avoid incurring additional charges.

If the holder fails to pay the defined minimum portion of the debt, the issuer will impose penalties such as late fees.

To mitigate this, financial institutions often organize for automatic payments. Through automatic payments, the monthly payment is deducted from the user's bank account. As long as the user has enough funds, automatic payments help the cardholder mitigate penalties and additional fees.

Also, as of today, many banks offer electronic statements so you can access your bill anytime as soon as it's released. This serves as an addition if not a replacement to physical statements.

Electronic statements can be checked by logging in to the user's account on the issuer's online banking site. The notification for every new statement is sent to the user's email address.

If the issuer allows it, the user can have other options such as electronic fund transfer for paying the debt apart from a physical check. Depending on the card issuer, the user can also make multiple payments during one billing cycle.

Please, leave a review for this book on Amazon

Credit Card Pros and Cons

Pros

Why should you get one? Here are some reasons.

1. More purchasing options

The use of cash is often only limited to in-person purchases unless, of course, you choose the Cash on Delivery option when ordering a product online. With a credit card, you can order via the internet or the phone.

2. Convenience

Credit cards are more convenient to use compared to cash and checks. You don't have to bring a ton of cash with you when shopping and by just swiping your card, you are done with a transaction. In metropolitan areas, cities, and suburban towns, many establishments accept credit cards. This implies that you need not stop by an ATM to pay for what you need. However, there are places that don't allow customers to give tip via a credit card.

3. Pay in Installments

While it's advised to pay your debt fully each month, you can pay your balance in installments over a specified period of time. It's useful when you find yourself short of money.

4. Build credit

If you use your credit card correctly, which means paying on time, maintaining the minimum balance, and keeping your balance low, among others you can build a good credit score. (More on this in the next section). A good credit score is useful when you need to apply for an auto loan or when you need financing to buy a house or start a business.

5. Emergency funds

Using credit cards to cover emergency expenses is not recommended. However, there are times that a credit card can cover small unexpected expenses, which is especially handy if you don't have enough savings.

6. Earn rewards

If you pay on time and you don't incur penalties, you will earn rewards that you can utilize for gift cards, credit card miles, or cash. You can earn rewards by using your credit card often and by paying on time. Nonetheless, this should never be the sole reason for getting a card.

Please, leave a review for this book on Amazon

7. All the perks of using plastic without paying interest charges

Some credit cards have 0% interest on balance transfers and purchases for the first six months. This enables you to pay your debt over time without incurring additional charges. In addition, if you settle your total balance each month, you can enjoy the convenience and flexibility that credit cards offer without worrying about interest fees.

8. No loss of access to funds

If someone accesses your checking account without authorization, they can drain all the balance in it. In this case, you must wait for a certain period of time for the processing of your fraudulent report before you receive your lost funds. With a credit card, you must wait for the processing period also. But at least, you can access your account and still make purchases using your credit card.

9. You have the right to withhold payment

There are times when credit card users experience some type of billing error. This can include unauthorized charges. Unauthorized charges may include a charge that is listed on your monthly account statement with the wrong amount or date, a charge for an item that was not delivered. You may receive a billing error when the issuer fails to update a payment made by you. When you experience this, you have the right to file a report. You can dispute it with the issuer. Meanwhile, you need not pay for the error.

Cons

Using a credit card has many benefits, but there are some downsides, namely:

1. Uncontrolled spending

A credit card gives people the illusion that they have more money than what they really have. It encourages many people to spend more than they can afford.

It gives you additional purchasing power, so you might be tempted to buy things that are out of your league.

Studies showed that credit card holders are more willing to go over their balance than other people.

2. Reduce future income

Each time you apply for a loan or each time you use your credit card, you are borrowing money with interest. You haven't earned that money yet, and you are obliged to pay it in the future. A small portion or a large chunk of your income may go towards the payment for your credit card balance.

Please, leave a review for this book on Amazon

3. It can be confusing

For people who are totally new to credit card agreements, the terms and conditions can be confusing. If you plan to become a credit card holder, you must understand the technical terms so that you can use it correctly and be free from penalties.

4. Interest and fees are expensive

Depending on the type of credit card you have and on the way you utilize it, you may incur hundreds of dollars' worth of interest and fees during the course of one year. This is the reason why you have to understand credit card terms and to know how to avoid penalties and fees.

5. Credit card fraud

Owning a credit card makes you vulnerable to credit card fraud. Thieves and hackers don't need to steal your card to acquire your information and use your balance. By hacking the online shop where you have used your card, they can steal your personal information. They can use it to purchase goods or services. They get the item while you receive the debt.

6. You pay without cash but you generate debt

Each time you avail or purchase something using a credit card, you generate debt. And each time you miss a due date, your debt increases.

7. Misuse ruins your credit score

Your credit score is directly tied to how you utilize your credit card. If you fail to meet agreements, your credit score is affected.

8. How are they useful when trying to build a credit score?

Lenders perform a valuation of their clients so that they can determine whether or not a client can avail a particular loan such as an auto or mortgage loan or be able to repay his or her debts. They need to know your creditworthiness.

Your credit score evaluates your creditworthiness. It is based on your credit history, which in turn reflects your ability to pay.

Now, at the beginning, you probably won't have any credit score from FICO. After all, you won't have any record with the credit Bureau if you have not engaged in any traceable transaction that can serve as proof that you can pay loans.

By getting a credit card, you can get started. Credit card companies will report your payment activity to the credit bureau. Remember that payment history makes up 35% of FICO scores and you can start getting that good payment history going by using your credit card and paying your monthly credit card dues.

Please, leave a review for this book on Amazon

If you already have a credit score albeit a poor one and you want to show the credit bureaus that you've steered your finances back on track, you can start by using your credit card and then paying your bills diligently. In just a few years, you will be able to start building that credit.

To build credit with your credit card, remember to:

- Pay in full and on time
- Treat your credit card as a debit card
- Remember to keep your balance low
- Keep your accounts open

All these tips are in keeping with the principles that help you keep healthy credit.

Types of Credit Cards

The first credit cards made during the 1950s had 1 feature only – they allow you to carry out business with an establishment and then get a monthly bill, much like utilities. They were also initially offered only to the wealthy.

Nowadays, credit cards are distinct from each other in many ways. Each type may differ from another when it comes to fees, rewards programs, and interest rates.

Before choosing your credit card, it's crucial to know the best one for your lifestyle and financial situation.

1. Vanilla credit cards

Vanilla credit cards are also known as standard credit cards. It has no special features, perks, or annual fee. Its credit limit depends on the user's creditworthiness. This is ideal for students, new credit card users and low-income individuals.

Pros

- Cheaper than other cards
- Simple and easy to use
- Easy to apply
- Low interest rate

Please, leave a review for this book on Amazon

Cons

- Not flexible

- Usually no additional offers or features

2. Reward Cards

Reward cards are credit cards that offer incentives to purchase certain products or services. You get points for every dollar spent and you can exchange them for rewards, hence the name. They are usually made accessible through a store or group of stores that allows clients to get price reductions according to the amount that they spend.

These cards are ideal for frequent travellers and those who like shopping. There are many kinds of rewards cards and the 5 most common are:

- Cash back cards,

- General reward points cards,

- Retail rewards cards,

- Gas cards, and

- Travel credit cards.

Cardholders don't have to settle for just one rewards credit card. Having more than one card in your wallet gives you the opportunity to earn more rewards. It is wise to have one credit card that pays high rewards on gas purchases and another one for travel purchases.

Pros

- Earn points while spending

- Travel for free

- Enjoy exclusive perks

Cons

- High interest rates

- High annual fees

How to travel for free using your credit card

You can charge the travel expenses on the card and redeem the travel points as statement credits. You can also use cashback (i.e. earn back a certain percentage of the money you spend on your credit card) to pay for the travel expenses. Earn enough travel points and cashback and it is possible to travel for free

Here are the steps to take and the tips to remember in order to travel for free using your credit card.

1. Apply for the right credit card.

This means that you will likely need a good credit score and if you don't have that, refer to our guide on how to achieve a good credit score. We also have a guide on how to climb the credit card ladder in the next chapter.

Go for a reward credit card with no cap as to the reward points you can earn. Ideally, the reward points should not have an expiration period, or at least have a longer expiration period. Keep an eye out for perks such as **complimentary companion tickets** and **waived baggage fees**.

There are generally two types of travel credit cards. **General purpose** credit cards give high rewards on all kinds of travel expenses, while **brand-specific** cards offer excellent rewards only when paying for the services of specific airlines or hotels. If you're loyal to a certain airway or hotel, you may want to choose the latter.

You'll probably have to pay an annual fee on the best travel rewards credit cards. Many cards don't have an annual fee in the first year, but starting in year two, you'll have to pay the fee. If you can earn enough rewards for a free flight or hotel, you'll hardly notice that you've paid the annual fee. If you do end up having to pay fees, make sure you pay them off right away, so you don't pay any interest on the annual fee.

2. Charge everything to your card.

Here's how you can get as many rewards points as possible – pay for everything with your card, including your groceries and other expenses – even utilities. Use it as much as you can. This doesn't mean that you should spend more than you can. In fact, you should only spend within your means. It only means that whenever you have to pay for something, use your cards.

3. Meet the minimum spending requirement

This is why the first tip is important. Some of the best rewards cards have minimum spending requirements. The Chase Sapphire Preferred card, for example, requires that you charge at least $3000 during the first 3 months!

Now, for many people, spending $3000 in three months just to get free flights just isn't feasible. The good news is that it's not as difficult as it looks. You can use your credit card to pay for a lot of things including utilities, taxes, and several months' worth of your insurance premiums in advance. You can buy gift cards at Amazon and then "sell" them to friends or use them further down the line.

You can even ask the company you work for if you can use your personal credit card for business expenses and then just have them reimburse you. You can also tell trustworthy friends and family that if they're looking to buy things, you'd appreciate if they'd use your card and then just reimburse you.

3. Join many rewards and frequent flyers programs

You can also enrol in airline and hotel loyalty programs. These will also pay rewards for your flights and stays. Enrolling is free. You just have to remember to use your loyalty program number when you book and charge to your credit card for more reward points.

They won't cost anything except perhaps a few minutes of your time. This doesn't mean you should scour the web for all rewards programs and sign up for every single one.

Start with your favorite service providers and if you have little travel experience, then start with what you're planning on your trip. Before you even book a flight and hotel rooms in your target destination, join the rewards programs of brands you're looking to spend for.

4. Enjoy your signup bonus

Find out if the credit card you applied for comes with a great sign up bonus. Collecting the bonus can be as easy as using the card to make a purchase within the first 3 months or paying the annual fee. It's a really good deal if the sign up bonus is higher than the annual fee.

5. Always pay your balance in full

This is one of the most crucial rules to follow when you're using any type of rewards credit card, especially when you are using a travel rewards card.

Paying your balance in full each month can help you increase your credit score. This will allow you to measure up for better credit card offers. Having a good credit score is crucial, but that's not the only reason to pay your balance in full each month.

It is important to pay finance charges on time since it cancels out the rewards obtained on the credit card. This happens when you carry a balance on your credit card beyond the time frame for payment.

6. Redeem your rewards right away

You can either use your rewards to book travel via the card's online booking tool, or you can redeem your rewards for a statement credit to reduce the amount that you owe. If you choose the statement credit option, you'll have to charge the expense of the travel to your credit card, and then, you have to use your rewards to credit the account for the travel expenses.

Please, leave a review for this book on Amazon

If you don't want to end up paying off the balance, exchange your rewards right away. Otherwise, you might have to pay at least the minimum payment to keep your account in good standing while you wait for the statement credit to post to your account.

7. Pay on time to avoid forfeiting your rewards

The fine print of your rewards credit card includes the things that can make you lose your credit card rewards. Most commonly, late payments can cost you all the points you've collected. It is the last thing you want after you've worked so hard to collect rewards.

3. Student credit cards

Card issuers market student credit cards to students and to people who have not yet owned a credit card. Student credit cards allow new users to establish a good credit history. It can help them in securing a car loan or an apartment in the future.

Pros

- Available for those with no credit score
- Easy to apply for
- No cash deposits required

Cons

- Interest rates can be high
- Low credit limit

4. Charge cards

Charge cards have no interest. But these types of payment cards require you to pay your balance fully every month. An uncapped credit limit is a feature of charge cards. In addition to that, charge cards come with generous rewards and benefits. However, their annual fee is high. It can range from $120 to $550.

This kind of credit card is best for high-income people.

Pros

- May allow unlimited spending
- You can acquire purchase points

Please, leave a review for this book on Amazon

- You can obtain points on travel and dining expenses
- Generous rewards
- It's flexible

Cons

- Missed payments can affect your credit score tremendously
- Need to pay in fully per month

5. Secured credit cards

Secured credit cards are credit cards that the cardholder guarantees with a safety deposit which is often tantamount to the entire line of credit. These cards usually have a controlled line of credit and come with an annual fee. After continual, responsible use, the issuer will return the security deposit. These cards may likewise be known as paid credit cards and semi-secured credit cards.

This kind of credit card is best for those with no or poor credit history.

Pros

- Available for credit newbies
- It can help you re-establish your credit scores
- Earn interest on your deposits
- Issuers report to credit bureaus

Cons

- The need for cash deposits

6. Sub-prime credit cards

A person with a sub-prime credit has a credit record that is too weak to be given rewards. Typically, sub-prime credit cards have high-interest rates. They also come with low credit limits and extra fees. This type of credit card is ideal for new users and individuals with a credit score of less than 600.

Pros

- Available for credit newbies
- Easy to apply for

Cons

- Unsecured
- With cash deposits

7. Prepaid cards

Prepaid cards are related to secured credit cards, but such cards are not linked to any bank account. In general, when you utilize a prepaid credit card, you are spending money that you have loaded onto the card. This is ideal for those who'd like to do some online shopping and those who want a convenient option to pay for travel deals.

Pros

- Available for consumers with damaged credit
- Available for credit newbies

Cons

- Require security deposits
- Have high percentage rates
- Does not help build credit score
- Has application fees
- With cash deposits

8. Limited purpose cards

Limited purpose cards are credit cards that can be used at a store or in fast-food chains. Limited purpose credit cards are accessible so it's ideal for new users, people who own small businesses who need supplies, shoppers, travelers, and sub-prime users.

Pros

- Available for credit newbies

Please, leave a review for this book on Amazon

- Freebies
- No need for security deposit

Cons
- With cash deposits
- Not flexible

9. Business credit cards

Business credit cards are designed to cover business expenses. They are not made for personal use. They help businesses in building a credit profile. This is for the purpose of improving future credit borrowing terms. They're discussed in detail in Chapter 10.

Pros
- Easy access to a revolving LOC
- Quickly access financing for short-term needs
- Increase the purchasing power of your company

Cons
- Has high-interest charges
- Limited balance

Basic Features of Credit Cards

Every credit card these days come with the following:

- **Purchase Rate**

    This is the interest rate that is applied to the charges you've made to your credit card. Note that this only applies to the balances that you were unable to pay in full by the end of your billing cycle that is already outside of the grace period. In the next section, you'll know more about this.

- **Credit limit**

    The issuer determines the credit limit set on the credit card. There are two types of credit limit.

Normal credit limit is the usual credit provided by the lending institution during the issuance of the credit card.

The revolving credit limit depends on how the card is used and on what items or services are purchased or availed.

- **Can be used to pay in foreign and domestic currency**

  Credit cards give you the ability to pay for goods and services in either domestic or foreign currency. With this feature, you can pay merchants in any part of the world.

- **All transactions are recorded**

  Lending institutions, like NBFCs or banks, record all of their credit card holder's transactions. The records help the entities to bill their credit card holders appropriately.

- **Service Fees**

  In the course of owning a credit card, you will encounter different kinds of credit card fees. These include balance transfer fees, one time processing fee, and credit limit increase fees.

  To know more about these, take a close look at your credit card agreement.

- **Regular charges**

  Issuers charge basic charges routinely as opposed to service fees that only occur when certain circumstances arise. Regular fees are nominal in nature, and there are two types of them: Annual charges and Additional charges. The latter are collected for supplementary services such as the issue of a new credit card.

- **Grace period**

  As mentioned before, the grace period is the period in which you won't incur financial and interest charges while carrying a balance. It's basically the amount of time you have before your new purchases start incurring charges. In the US, regulations dictate that consumers be given at least 21 days to pay before their purchase start incurring interest. You can find the length of your grace period on the back or front of your billing statement.

- **Service tax**

  This is always included in the amount charged to the borrower. The service tax is mandatory. Because of this, the final end cost paid by the user increases. Many issuing entities set policies that reverse the service tax that is charged on fuel, gas, and goods purchases.

Please, leave a review for this book on Amazon

- **Gifts, bonus points, and other offers**

    Conventionally, offering incentives is a trendy way to improve sales. Credit card providers also use this tactic when they market their credit cards. Therefore, card providers often give rewards, gifts, and bonus points to their cardholders. By accumulating bonus points, you can redeem cash back offers, gifts, and other rewards. To be eligible for many rewards, you may have to use your credit card frequently.

Factors to Consider When Choosing a Credit Card

A credit card is a handy tool for many occasions. However, it can inflict terrible damage to your life, budget, and monthly salary if you misuse it or choose the wrong type.

Not all credit cards are created equal. Here are some of the things you need to check when looking for a credit card

1. Interest rates

The Annual Percentage Rate is the interest rate that you have to pay yearly. The APR is an important factor to consider in comparing credit cards.

To compute the APR, multiply the monthly rate by twelve. The product, at times, is not what it appears to be. There are also introductory rates, which are also known as teaser rates. They are considered as interest rates that are charged to a client during the initial stages of a loan.

Depending on the financial institution, the teaser rate can be as low as 0%. It's not permanent and it expires after a specific period of time. The value of the rate depends on the card's balance.

Other than teaser rates, there are other types of rates that apply to transactions made using the card. The rates depend on the type of transaction and on how the cardholder uses his or her credit card. For example, cash advances have high-interest rates, and apart from the APR, other rates apply to balance transfers.

You have to check the clauses on the agreement regarding the card's APR in order to know whether the deal is good in the long term or not. People often read the short term deals only. They fail to check the other provisos included in a contract. For your best interest, you must read everything carefully.

Furthermore, APRs are either variable or fixed. This means that they either depend on the prime rate or remain constant. The prime rate is the interest rate that issuers lend to their prime customers – the most creditworthy ones. Variable-rate credit cards are pegged to the prime rate. The APR of variable-rate credit cards can change. It is usually tied to an index.

Being a benchmark rate, an index is considered as the LIBOR or the prime rate. For instance, if it is stated in the agreement that the APR is prime plus 10% and the benchmark rate is at 5%, the credit card's interest rate is 15%.

As a further matter, you have to understand what the lending institution will charge you aside from the prime rate and whether the company can change the rate or not.

2. Grace period or billing cycle

The billing cycle determines when you should start paying interest on the purchases that you make using your credit card. It's advised to choose a credit card that offers a long grace period.

3. Fees

Most credit cards have annual fees. Annual fees are not always that bad, especially if you are paying the annual fee to acquire something that can benefit you. For example, some credit cards offer a lot of miles or travel points even though their annual fee is higher than others. Flyer miles are part of an airline or a financial institution's loyalty program.

When choosing from different types of credit cards, be sure to check their fees and to see the rewards you can get from the credit cards with high annual fees. Also, if there is no fee, check the APR. It can be higher than others. Furthermore, transferring your balance to another payment card or taking cash advances can also make you incur additional fees.

4. Expiry dates and special offers

Some lending companies offer special APR, cash advance rates, and balance transfer fees. You have to make sure to check the expiry dates of these offers.

In every credit card agreement, the APR is presented as a certain percentage. If you see an asterisk or any sign beside the APR, you must thoroughly read the fine print.

5. Penalties and Minimums

Lenders require users to pay a minimum portion of the debt every month. It can either be a flat fee or a percentage. If you don't pay the monthly fee before the due date, the company will charge you with a penalty fee. If it will be hard for you to pay a fixed amount per month, choose the credit card that has no non-payment fee or the one that offers the lowest limit.

Please, leave a review for this book on Amazon

6. Rewards and Points

Most credit cards offer rewards and points for utilizing them. Excellent rewards often come with a fee. There are no-fee credit cards that offer rewards and points too. Once you've chosen a credit card that offers the best deals on fees, grace period, and interest rates, check the rewards and points that you can get.

7. Specialization

Some credit cards are designed for shoppers, travelers, business people, students etc. Thus, you must choose the type that is right for your needs. For example, the credit cards tailored for students have low spending limits and low fees.

In a similar way, credit cards that are designed for wealthy consumers have low APR but the credit limit is high. Cards designed for travelers offer redeemable points for flights and other bonus points, but its annual fee may be high.

8. Credit limit

The credit limit of your chosen type of credit card must cover your needs. The amount must be enough to provide flexibility, but it must not be higher than what you can afford to pay.

Low-limit cards are perfect for college students, whereas high limit cards are tailored for business people and wealthy folks. Remember that spending a low percentage of your credit limit per month is one of the best ways to increase your credit score.

Whether you want to upgrade your credit card or you are applying to get one for the first time, keep those factors in mind.

Ways to Avoid a Finance Charge on Your Credit Card

Finance charges are calculated based on recent purchases and unpaid balance so when you're late in paying the minimum monthly payment, you will incur finance charges. A finance charge is compensation to the lending institution for extending credit or for providing the funds to a borrower.

The single most effective way to avoid finance charges is to pay your balance on time. Don't settle for paying the minimum. Note that finance charges are used by card issuers to charge their customers for carrying a balance, so the best way to avoid them is to refrain from carrying a balance

Please, leave a review for this book on Amazon

in the first place. Paying your balance fully before the end of every billing cycle prevents you from incurring finance charges.

Remember that every credit card has a grace period. Typically, it is between 21 and 25 days. During the grace period, you do not incur finance charges. So to pay zero finance charges, pay your credit balance fully during the grace period.

You may also transfer your balance to another card to dodge additional charges. This is recommended if you can't pay your balance in full within the grace period. Consider transferring your balance to another card with low APR. For instance, some credit cards give you zero percent APR for a specific period.

By transferring your credits, you can, in a way, get rid of your balance cheaply. However, keep in mind that you can't do that forever. Transferring your balance may also come with fees plus you will still have to pay for that amount in the credit card you transferred it to.

Finally, be wary of promos. When the 0% APR promo expires, you are obliged to pay a higher interest rate than before, so be sure to read and complete the terms and conditions of the agreement.

There is a database in which you can read and check out all the different credit card agreements available from various companies online. It's available on the site of the Consumer Financial Protection Bureau. You can check the list out at www.consumerfinance.gov. Do your research and you'll be spared from a lot of headache.

Did You Know?

The FICO score is based on the behavior of millions of borrowers. The model looks for patterns in behavior that indicates a borrower might default, as well as patterns that indicated a borrower is likely to pay.

Please, leave a review for this book on Amazon

Chapter 9

How To Climb The Credit Card Ladder

Credit cards are a good way to build or repair credit scores and as you get better scores, you'll find yourself being able to apply for better cards.

You'll start from the basic cards with no benefits and eventually get to enjoy credit cards with amazing cash back offers. You might even end up with prestigious cards that reward you with international lounge access. Or if you are an extremely high earner, you can avail of invite only cards available to the wealthy.

Each credit card tier has corresponding credit score and income requirements. You do not have to aspire for the most premium card. The card you choose to start with and then upgrade to should suit your long-term needs and your income status at the time.

Tier 1

This is where you'll find the starter cards. Those who are beginning to build their credit score or improving it are recommended to start with these cards. These are great for students, people with bad credit score, and immigrants just started settling in US. Some of Tier 1 credit cards have annual fees. There are also no rewards, cashback, and airline miles.

Student cards

Students can start using credit card and begin to establish credit score. After some time, the feature of these cards can include cashback and rewards program. Generally, you should be a student to be eligible to avail this card.

Basic or secured cards

This is a no-frills credit card. Non-students should apply for a secured card. Like the students cards, this can also level up to cards with more useful features.

Interestingly, Discover is the only major credit card issuer that offers cashback for secured cards. But Discover is not honored at every establishment. In the event that your Discover card is declined, pay with a debit card. Also, you should not prioritize spending yet because the goal is to build credit and not earn points.

You should not concern yourself with interest rates and late fees either because you are expected to pay your balances in time and in full. Also, the credit limit should not matter because you are supposed to build your credit and not rely on the card often. But to be exact, the credit limit on these cards is based on the minimum or maximum deposits.

Please, leave a review for this book on Amazon

Secured cards require minimum deposits in case you are not able to pay the monthly bills. Capital One has the lowest minimum deposit at $49. Bank of America, US Bank, and Wells Fargo have the highest minimum deposit of $300. As for maximum deposit, it ranges from $2500 to $10000.

Not all secured credit cards have annual fees. Citi, Discover, and Capital One do not require annual fees. Wells Fargo, Bank of America and US Bank have annual fees of $25, $39, and $25, respectively.

If the card issuer upgrades the card to unsecured credit card, they might still charge annual fees. But you can talk to them about waiving the fee. One tip is to insinuate that you might close your accounts if you still have to pay the annual fee.

Product change is swapping a credit card to other cards in the issuer's portfolio. You can do this when you upgrade to an unsecured credit card. Bank of America requires that you deposited a considerable sum in their bank to access the valuable cards, otherwise, other card issuers have better choices. Capital One's best unsecured card may be the Quicksilver card that earns 1.5% on all purchases.

Citi has Costco card, Citi Double Cash card, and the Citi Dividend card that offer more than 2% cashback. US Bank has the US Bank Cash Card+ as the best option for cashback reward. Wells Fargo has an inconvenient inquiry process for product change. You may be better off choosing from the other issuers.

Subprime cards

If you do not qualify for the student and secured credit cards, you can opt to apply for a subprime card. However, these are not very practical because they incur high fees. They have a monthly fee but no benefits to speak of. Subprime cards should be your last resort.

You might be tempted to get these because of very little requirements and that there's no deposit needed. However, they are not valuable and will be costly to keep in the long run.

Whichever tier 1 credit card you choose, it is advisable to keep using the card for 6 to 12 months before upgrading to a higher level one. Keep in mind that you are building or improving your credit score. Practice responsible use of these cards. You should have accumulated a credit score of more than 650 before moving on the next tier.

A technique you can use to increase our credit score is to prepay your cards. Do not max them out but leave a small balance to decrease utilization. Of course, you should pay the full balance after the statement closes.

Tier 2

When you finally graduate to a higher tier card, these can further establish the foundation of your credit score. You can now begin earning rewards by optimizing points. You can get reward points or cash back with your purchases. These cards also offer sign up bonuses.

Please, leave a review for this book on Amazon

One of the most common kinds is the travel rewards card. But be careful with this because it's pointless to optimize for free travel or other rewards by accruing tons of debt.

The credit limit on these cards ranges from $500 to $10000. In order to avail one, you have to have a credit score of 690 to 720. You will be also asked to provide a proof of income.

Cashback cards are some of the more common cards under this category. With these cards, you get a small amount of money back by charging purchases to your credit card, hence the name. You redeem it by deducting your cashback from the statement balance, deposit in a bank account, or redeem as gift cards.

Cashback comes in different modes: flat percentage, bonus category, and tiered rewards. Flat percentage cashback credit cards earn the same rebate with every spending. It appeals to the busy, straightforward consumers. Bonus category and tiered reward cards entail strategic purchasing but earn bigger cashback. These are for people who do not mind planning their spending to get more cashback.

Cashback rewards overweigh the banks interest rate. For example, with a low bank interest rate, you can only earn 0.6% annual yield with a usual savings account. You will earn better returns with at least 1% cashback on purchases. Cashback is also tax-free.

Travel benefits are other main rewards on higher tier credit cards. You can travel for free if you save enough points to redeem rewards. Use your credit card on all travel-related purchases. You also have to pay your full balance every month. That way, there will be no interest fee and no late fees to pay off. Plus, you may lose your saved points if you are late in paying your balances.

Tier 2 Cards Worth Taking a Look At

If you want to save travel points, Chase has the best travel cards available. You can start with their cards. However, Chase has a 5/24 rule. If you apply for one of their cards, you will be rejected if you have 5 new cards in your credit report for the past 24 months.

Chase Freedom credit cards

These cards can accumulate Ultimate Rewards (UR) which is transferrable to a higher tier Chase card to optimize reward redemption. Chase Freedom has a $150 sign up bonus after spending $500 in 3 months. It also has a 5% cashback on various categories that change every quarter. Cashback is applicable up to $1500 in combined spending. It requires activation every quarter.

Chase Freedom Unlimited

This one has the same sign up bonus but offers 1.5% cashback on all purchases. Both credit cards offer sign up bonus of 15,000 UR points. If you get a higher level card, the Chase Sapphire Reserve for instance, you will a get better optimization of reward points upon redemption.

Discover It

This has 5% cashback on changing categories each quarter, up to $1500 value of combined purchases. It has cashback match of 10% in the first year. The card also offers attractive Discover Deals where you can use the cashback match. However, there are a few cons for the issuer, like Discover removing long term insurance options for their credit cards. This means, Discover cards would not be recommended if you intend on long-standing warranty or return protection for long term purchases.

Discover It Miles

On the other hand, this card offers 1.5% cashback on every purchase, 3% cashback match for the first year which is usable on Discover Deals.

US Bank Cash+ credit card

This one has cashback offer with the added perk of being able to choose the rotating categories each quarter. The card offers 5% cashback on 2 chosen categories, until $2000 in combined spending. It also has 2% cashback on everyday purchase category such as groceries, gas, or restaurants, and 1% cash back on other purchases.

The American Express Blue Cash Everyday

With this card, you can enjoy a 3% cashback on grocery store purchases, maximum of $6000 worth of spending. It also has 2% cashback at gas station spending and selected department stores, and 1% cashback on anything else. This card earns cash back through statement credits.

Amex Everyday

This one has Membership Reward (MR) Points. It earns twice the MR points at grocery stores up to $6000 on combined purchases. It also offers 1x MR points anywhere else. if you reached more than 20 transactions per billing, you also earn 20% bonus in MR points. If you want to earn travel rewards and availing an Amex Platinum or Amex PRG soon, it is recommended you go for the Amex Everyday card.

Citi Double Cash card

If you want to eliminate having to deal with changing categories and thinking of which card to choose, you may opt for Citi Double Cash card. It offers 2% cashback on every purchase. You can also earn an additional 1% cashback when you pay the balance of said purchases. You can redeem cashback as a check, gift card, or statement credit.

Please, leave a review for this book on Amazon

Citi Bank cards offer perks such as Return Guarantee and Price Protection. They also have Citi Private Pass which can be valuable in availing Citi's presale or exclusive passes. It covers the best in dining, live music, family entertainment, dining, among others.

Choosing and using a Tier 2 Card

Choose a card with no annual fees. Any card issuer should be glad to have your business especially since at this point, you have proven that you are a responsible cardholder.

Remember to keep paying your balances in full every time to avoid interest payment and to maintain good credit.

Avoid cash advances and balance transfers. They incur extra charges and do not give you any rewards. These also lessen the available credit you can use towards earning rewards.

Take advantage of the sign up bonus, there are great ones like free flight. You have to spend a set amount on the card within the first three months of getting it. Pick a card with a sign up bonus that is easy to redeem. The minimum purchase should be manageable for you to pay off each month.

Take note that when you upgrade to tier 3 card, you should still keep your tier 2 card. They are now called anchor cards. These increase your score in the long run. It is better if the tier 2 card has no annual fee. Just make sure to charge purchases on it every 5 months to keep it active.

Tier 3

These credit cards have better benefits than tier 2 cards. They may have annual fees or not. If carrying an annual fee, the value of rewards should be greater than the annual fee. Most of its perks are travel-related. It also has a more attractive sign up bonus.

Annual fees of tier 3 cards are priced at $65 minimum. To get one of these cards, you should have a credit score ranging from 710 to 740. You also have to show that you are earning close to $61,000 per year while having a good credit history.

Because you get this card for the rewards, you have to compare its cost and benefits. For example, the Chase Hyatt card offers free overnight stay every year. This certainly outweighs the annual payment of $75.

When choosing a tier 3 card, you have to consider also the hidden cost along with the obvious cost. This is the same for main benefits and hidden benefits. You can think of the annual fees as the main cost and opportunity cost as the hidden cost. And sign up bonuses and points earned are the main benefits while improving the credit score criteria is a hidden benefit.

Please, leave a review for this book on Amazon

Cards carrying annual fees have sign up bonuses. You can also earn points on chosen categories that have purchase multipliers. The hidden benefit of using the card is the improvement of the credit score criteria such as number of accounts given that you pay the full balance in time monthly and also the average of accounts.

If you are after travel perks, a good option to consider may be Citi Prestige. It has an annual fee is $450 and a sign-up bonus of $250 in travel credit. The next thing to think about is can you get $200 worth or more from other benefits. The other rewards include Priority Pass, Global Entry or TSA Pre-check credit, 3-hour trip delay protection, and 4th night free hotel stay.

The 4th night free benefit can be used multiple times a year. You can get at least $200 worth just using this perk alone. For instance, you can plan to take four vacations of at least 4 days in one year. You have four nights free. Thinking in terms of cost, if the price is $100 per night, you can have $400 in savings. If the price is $200 a night, you can save $800.

If you want to optimize rewards and receive benefits worth more than the card costs, you have to spend a bit of time to think of the positive value of using the card. And what kind of benefits are you really looking after and will you be actually able to use the rewards. Only then, will keeping a rewards-heavy card be worth it.

Tier 4

For those who earn good income regularly, this is most prestigious card. Benefits include access to airport lounges around the world. These carry higher annual fees that range from $400 to $550. You can also add additional cardholders. Adding additional users means additional annual fees up to $175 each cardholder.

To be eligible for tier 4 credit cards, you should have a credit score of at least 730. If you have a score lower than 730, you should be earning $61,000 or more per year. Or you can have a lower income but you should have a good credit history and high score. You will get the most of these cards if you are a frequent flyer.

They also have higher spending multiplier than tier 3 credit cards. Chase Sapphire, for instance, earns 3 times on travel purchases. It also has $300 travel credit, $100 Global Entry/TSA Precheck Credit, and unlimited Priority Pass Access.

Not all cards have fees for additional cardholders. Hilton Amex Aspire, Delta Reserve Card, SPG Luxury Card, and United Club Card do not carry annual fees for additional users. Moreover, Hilton Amex Aspire offers $100 property credit for additional users that can used for 2-night stay at Conrad properties and Waldorf Astoria.

Please, leave a review for this book on Amazon

Amex Platinum has a sign-up bonus of 60,000 Membership Rewards (MR) points ($1140 value) which is redeemable after spending $5,000 in charged purchasing in the first 90 days. Hilton Amex Aspire offers $150,000 Hilton Honor (HH) points (worth $900) after spending $4000 in purchases during the first 90 days. Chase Sapphire Reserve has a sign-up bonus of $50,000 in Ultimate Rewards (UR) points (worth $1050) upon charging a $4000 worth of purchases in the first 3 months.

Amex Platinum earns 5 MR points per dollar spent on airfare-related purchases and prepaid hotel stays booked through the airline or Amex. There is 1 MR point for other spending. Hilton Amex Aspire offer 4 HH points per dollar spent on Hilton-owned properties internationally, 7 HH points per dollar spent on airline tickets booked through the airline or Amex, on car rentals booked directly with the participating companies, and purchases on US restaurants. They offer 3 HH points on other purchases. Chase Sapphire rewards has 3 UR points per dollar spent on dining and travel purchases, and 1 UR point for all other spending.

In choosing a Tier 4 card or cards, weigh the combination of rewards that would suit you best. Especially since the competition among these premium travel cards intensified with the enhanced benefits.

Tier 5

This is the invite-only credit card. Among these cards are the American Express Centurion and JPMorgan Chase Reserve. You are eligible for the JPMorgan Reserve if you have around $10 million managed by JPMorgan. To qualify for the American Express Centurion, you should have a $16 million net worth and yearly earnings of $1.3 million. Amex Centurion carries a $2500 annual fee and a $7500 signup fee.

These exclusive credit cards have lavish perks. For example, the American Centurion cardholders enjoy no credit limit, Membership Reward points, and exclusive upgrades and benefits to dining, travel, entertainment and more. The other benefits are still shrouded in mystery.

Another Tier 5 card, the Dubai First Royale Mastercard card comes with the services of a relationship manager that caters to the owner's specific whims. The manager also assists the cardholder book private getaways and vacations. This card is known as one of the most exclusive in the world. You have to be based in Dubai

Please, leave a review for this book on Amazon

Chapter 10

Business Credit Cards

Whenever you attempt to open up a new business, you will need some funding to cover a lot of its initial expenses. Your personal credit card will be sufficient to start the business but only to a point. If the business you are planning to set up is of a certain size, you might want to apply for a business credit card.

What are business credit cards and what makes them different?

A business credit card shares mostly the same functions with a typical personal credit card. You use them to make transactions and pay for the charges each card makes at the end of the month. However, there are certain aspects that make a business credit card considerably different from your typical card.

1. It's Not Covered by Most Consumer Protection Laws

This is quite simple: under the law, businesses are of a different category from what you will call "consumers". Sure, you can tell yourself that you yourself are a consumer but the credit card was issued for the legal entity that makes up your business.

This means that certain consumer protection laws like the Credit Card Act of 2009 won't apply to you as the card holder. This could lead to a number of problems which will include sudden shifts in that card's Annual Percentage Rate, even overnight at some instances, and charges for penalties and fees that border on being expensive and unreasonable.

However, there is a silver lining to all of this. If your business is quite small, some consumer protection laws might be extended to you. This is not true for all issuers so it's best not to expect to be covered once you are issued the card.

2. It Affects All Credit, Both Business and Personal

When it comes to being a business owner, the distinction between your personal credit and the business's credit is often blurred. In other words, your personal credit can affect how the business itself can apply for and use credit.

For instance, when issuers look at your application for a business credit card, they would look at your personal information and check if you have what it takes to handle the kind of liabilities that their product entails. As such, poor financial management skills might affect your ability to secure a credit card for the business in the first place.

Please, leave a review for this book on Amazon

It also goes without saying that reporting your transactions to the reporting agencies can get mixed. For instance, you might get a credit report where your entries for both your personal and business transactions are made into your timeline. Of course, this means that any mark reported to that agency regarding your business credit card's transactions, whether good or bad, will affect your credit score.

3. Higher Credit Limits

Due to the fact that your business is going to make a lot of expenses, the starting credit limit for a business credit card tends to be higher compared to personal ones. As such, if you can expect your business to make a lot of notable transactions, it's best that you apply for a credit card for businesses so you don't max your cards out quickly.

Of course, the same things that affect your credit score as a private individual will also affect you as the business owner. Even with the higher credit limit, the system of credit utilization rates still apply. Any credit you have available on that card, then, will be compared to the credit that you actually use on a regular basis. Depending on the reporting agency, credit utilization may comprise 30% to 40% of your score.

If you are not the type to overly rely on your business credit card, this could be an advantage for you. The higher credit limit means that it will take several huge purchases for you to even reach the 30% threshold reporting agencies recommend credit card users stick to. So as long as your credit utilization is within 15% to 19%, your credit score should remain high.

4. Perks

Due to the fact that business cards are a bit more demanding to maintain, certain credit card issuers offer certain perks for those that do apply for such. The most common perks are discounts for payments of several utility services like electricity, Internet connection, and phone connection. Some issuers even provide discounts on Wi-Fi rates as well as office supplies which might be an advantage for businesses that rely a lot on these.

However, you might be more interested with flat-rate rewards programs where you can avail of certain bonuses every time you make a purchase with the card. It's best to consult with the issuer first before you submit your application so you know what rewards you can expect if you frequently use that card.

Personal vs. business: Which card should you choose?

As was stated, there is the option to use your personal credit card over a business credit card for most of your transactions. If you are still deciding whether to stick to your personal card or apply for a business card, there are certain factors that you should consider.

You might be better off with a business credit card if:

- You are a starting entrepreneur who wants to build your business's credit trustworthiness.
- You run a company whose expenses require a larger credit limit.
- Your expenses align most with reward categories that business cards offer.
- You no longer want to deal with low credit limits.

However, a personal credit card might be for you if:

- You run a sole proprietorship whose business expenses fall below the usual personal credit card limits.
- Your expenses do not align with the rewards program most business credit cards offer.
- You are not interested in building credit for the business.
- You are not the one who would apply for a business loan anytime in the future.

Who can apply for a business credit card?

Naturally, the first requirement you need to qualify for a business card is to have a business. So, if you don't have at least any form of business, does that mean that you are not qualified for a business credit card?

The answer, surprisingly, is no. You can actually qualify for a business credit card even if you are just interested in the rewards that these cards have.

The reason for this is quite simple: there is no strict definition as to what a "business" actually is. It could range from hawking wares at a flea market or running a corporation with a hundred employees in it. It doesn't even matter if your previous business experience involves setting up a lemonade stand outside your home.

So as long as the money you generated from your activities can be considered as business revenue, then you might find some use for a business credit card. Either way, the issuer will still look at your

Please, leave a review for this book on Amazon

personal credit information to see if you have what it takes to meet the demands that the card entails.

Types of Business Cards

There are several business cards that you can apply for. They have the same functions and requirements but they will carry certain features that make them ideal in a number of situations. They are as follows:

1. Business Credit Cards

These are your typical credit card and they function mostly the same with a personal card. They have a credit limit that dictates how much you can use the card every month as well as how much you pay.

Whenever your card makes a charge, you are obligated to pay the charge each billing cycle. This doesn't mean you have to immediately pay the amount in full as you can pay in installments. Although, this does mean that you carry the balance month for month i.e. you will have to deal with interest rates until that debt is settled.

However, this does allow for a small financial cushion that small business owners can depend on during tough times.

2. Business Charge Cards

Like the typical business card, charge cards have the same function as personal credit cards. However, they differ greatly in the aspect of credit limits since, basically, there is none.

Charge cards have something that is called as a "shadow" limit which tend to be higher than most credit card limits and can be flexible depending on the card holder's needs. They can also change depending on how often you use your card as well as the overall status of your credit history.

However, there is a catch: Going over the limit can cause your account to be frozen. Also, you can never carry your balance on a month to month basis. You'll have to pay the charge in full every billing period.

This card is recommended only for people who have full control over their spending habits. If you can spend only on what you can afford, this charge card might be ideal for you.

3. Secure Business Cards

This card is ideal for businesses with little personal credit or none at all. Think of it as a credit builder card, only for business owners.

Please, leave a review for this book on Amazon

How it works is quite simple. When you apply for this card, you are required to deposit a minimum amount. This could be in between $2,000.00 and $5,000.00, depending on the card and the issuer.

This amount serves as your credit line and you can use that to pay for anything related to the business. Either way, every payment for that balance will be reported by the issuer to the credit reporting agency.

This way, your business can build up on its credit within a year. However, it's important to note that only on-time payments will be reported. Any payment you miss will be a derogatory mark, defeating the purpose of the card.

How to get a business credit card

The process of securing your business's credit card is surprisingly easy. In fact, the process is quite similar to getting a personal credit card. However, there are differences in the details that you will submit to the issuing company. Since this is a business credit card, then it would be apparent that the issuer would ask information regarding your business.

The application form will include questions like:

- The legal name of the business

- Address

- The type of industry it belongs to. Some industries are considered high-risk and high-maintenance which could affect the approval of your application.

- The structure of the company whether you are a sole proprietorship, a partnership, or a corporation.

- The age of the business i.e. how long it has been operating.

- Number of people employed as well as the organizational structure.

- Annual revenue

- Estimated monthly expenditures and other finance-related matters.

It really depends on the institution as to what kind of information that they want from you. To make it easier on your part, it's best to look for the information on your part and prepare your documents and answers beforehand.

Please, leave a review for this book on Amazon

What you need to secure a quick approval

In the end, it is up to the discretion of the bank or any similar financial institution to decide whether or not to approve your application for a business credit card. To make them easily decide for your approval, there are a few things you have to do beforehand:

1. Have a Business

Although you don't exactly have to have a business to qualify for a business credit card, having one does tend to improve your odds of successfully securing one. The lending institution would most likely want to make sure that whatever credit or money you can secure through the card would be used to invest for an actual venture. One proof that you have a business is through securing an Employer's Identification Number from the Internal Revenue Service as well as opening a business account.

2. Have a Good to Excellent Personal Credit Score

Your personal credit score will actually influence how your application is going to be treated. That lender would have to make sure that you as the applicant have what it takes to meet the demands of the card.

For this, they would pull up a hard search on your personal credit history and look for any mark made regarding your financial activities. What one creditor would look for is different from another but it's safe to say that applicants with a history of on-time payments, good credit utilization rates, and minimal to no derogatory marks tend to have a better chance of getting their applications approved.

What transactions could the business credit card be used for?

There is actually no hard and fast rule as to where and how you should use your business's credit card. It has the same functions as your typical credit card albeit with a larger credit limit and a few more restrictions/obligations on your part.

The question, then, is not on where your business credit card will be the most applicable but on how to optimize its usage while minimizing the risks it entails. To do those, here are a few tips to keep in mind.

1. Keep Everything Strictly Within Business

Even if you are running a sole proprietorship, resist any urge to use that card to spend for personal concerns. Keeping your business expenses separate from your personal one is one way to keep track of your expenses and claim deductions when taxing season comes around.

Please, leave a review for this book on Amazon

If you authorize your employees to use the card also, give guidelines as to what will qualify as a business expense. Having a system set up where employees have to seek approval before using the card and furnish receipts is a good way of enforcing accountability and limiting the card's use.

2. Make a Policy

If you are running a corporation, chances are your partners will also want to have access to that card. This would be an opportunity for you to draft a policy on how to use that card.

Make it a point to show to everyone that the card is accessible but only if they meet certain conditions and follow the guidelines. The point here is to be as transparent as possible in telling your staff and your partners who can use the card and for what purposes.

3. Set Limits

The 30% rule for personal credit card utilization rates apply here as well. If possible, do not go beyond 30% of the available credit when using the card. If the limit is at $10,000.00, then your spending should not be over $3,000.00.

Of course, there is a chance when the policy you have set up would not work in all situations. Some authorized users for the card might have different purposes in mind for it. This is where a bit of creativity comes into play.

You might set different limits for each user but you must set other limiters as well. For example, one user might only access the card for a certain set of situations or you rotate possession of the card to the different users on a bi-weekly basis. The point is to make sure that nobody gets to use the card for too long to avoid abuses.

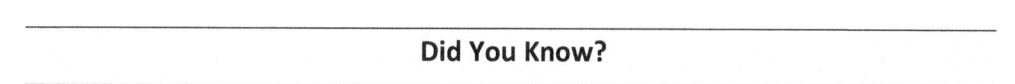

Did You Know?

If you pay your bill in full during the grace period, you won't have to pay a finance charge on purchases for that bill. A grace period is usually about 25 days.

Chapter 11

Credit Card Balance Transfer

Most people have been in that situation wherein expenses are suddenly crashing down on them all at the same time. To ease the cash flow, they turn to their credit cards for help. Before they knew it, they have maxed out the credit limit and are in even deeper trouble than they were before. But there might be a way to get out of this mess, and that is by taking advantage of credit card balance transfers.

Balance Transfer in a Nutshell

By the name itself, balance transfer is moving all of your outstanding balances from one or more of your credit card accounts to a new one with lower interest rates, fewer penalties, and more perks. Its main benefit is that you will be able to pay off the debt in fixed, monthly amounts with significantly reduced interest. It's very similar to paying a loan.

Through this option, you can save hundreds of dollars by simply moving all your credit card balances into a new credit card so you can manage your debt better. This works well if you're paying for a card that's almost maxed out, paying multiple credit cards at the same time, or just want to clear off your bills.

The interest rates depend on the length of the payment contract which can range from 6% up to 18.79% per year. So before you proceed with the transfer, you should compare rates and also ask for hidden fees required for the transfer especially if the credit card is from a different bank.

When Should You Do a Balance Transfer?

There are a couple of things you should consider before doing a credit card balance transfer.

First, you need to be absolutely committed to getting out of your credit card debt once and for all.

Since the balance transfer contract means you'll have to allot monthly amounts to pay off the loan. This will cut through your budget and you might just end up using your credit cards again. After all, it's easy to be tempted to use a zero balance credit card. To minimize the likelihood, you should reduce the number of cards you have. Start with those with annual fees and fewer perks. Although keeping card lines open makes your credit score healthy, the records for a closed credit card remains viable up to 10 years after the contract was terminated, so you should be good.

Second, you need to know your credit standing before you apply for a new card offering the balance transfer.

How extensive is your credit history? Longer is better, by the way. Have you ever been late for payment for more than 30 days? Are you almost maxed out on all your credit cards? You'll have a better chance of getting approved for a balance transfer if your total credit card debt is below 50%

of your credit cards' combined limit. This is referred to as the utilization ratio. Also, if your credit score is more than 720, you should be good to go. There will be approval doubts if you're between 660 and 720. Anything lower than 660 reduces the chances of getting a balance transfer approved significantly.

Pros and Cons of Balance Transfer

Pros

- Lower interest rates. This is the balance transfer's biggest draw, which is actually good especially if your current credit card has an insanely high interest rate. Lower interest rates mean you can reduce your credit balance card in less time.

- Better terms. Short grace period and high fees are just some of the terms your current credit card has committed you into. Your new credit card, however, may have better offerings aside from the balance transfer option like a better rewards system.

- Debt consolidation. If this new credit card has a high enough limit, you can transfer all your balances to this new account and get rid of the others. This way, you'll be able to manage your debt easier and you don't have to make separate payments to different banks.

Cons

- Higher interest rates. This usually happens if you're not qualified for the promotional interest rates. Qualifications were mentioned in the previous section. Basically, you need a good enough credit score to make the cut. Otherwise, you're stuck with the regular interest rates.

- Can get expensive. If the new credit card has annual fees and you also need to pay a balance transfer fee, you might end up paying more than working it out with your current credit card debts. Consider these amounts before you commit into balance transfer.

- More debt risks. Making sure that you don't get tempted to use your credit cards once you've cleared off the balances is a practice in discipline. That's because you have more credit available at your disposal. This can be good or bad depending on how you manage your finances.

Balance transfer may be worth it if, in the end, you'll be saving money and paying off your credit card balances. There are drawbacks and not all are entitled to this option.

Please, leave a review for this book on Amazon

Chapter 12

How to Protect Your Credit Card from Identity Theft

Identity theft is an existing crisis in the US that's continuing to grow every year. An Identity Theft Resource Center (ITRC) report is quite disturbing. It shows that 1,579 data breaches exposed about 179 million identity records in 2017.

Being a victim of an identity scam can cause you a lot of problems. One of the worst cases would be the downfall of your credit score.

How identity theft can ruin your credit score

The most common type of identity theft crime is credit card fraud. Fraudsters would steal your personal information and your credit card details. They would then use the stolen information for unauthorized transactions.

The fraudsters can either steal your credit card or perform a card-not-present fraud. But, they'd also need information such as your birthday and Social Security number.

You may end up with a credit card bill that you might not be able to pay or handle if you become a victim. This may affect your credit score if you don't act on it fast.

Ways to avoid becoming an identity theft victim

Proving that you're a victim of identity theft can be inconvenient. There's a long process to go through which involves a lot of documentation before you can prove your innocence.

It would still be best to avoid these kinds of troubles and there are several ways you can do it.

1. Watch out for Phishing Scams

A phishing scam is a criminal's method to get personal information such as passwords. The most common way of phishing is sent via e-mail.

These e-mails would look like official e-mails from a bank or other companies. The contents would often inform you about system changes or promotional offers. It would ask you to enter personal information because of these reasons. In some cases, these emails scare you into providing info by saying that that access to your account will be restricted if you don't "update" your account.

The e-mail would also contain an external link to a fraud web page that would look like the bank's legit website. Entering your personal details on this page will result in big problems for you. The criminals will use your details to perform transactions under your name.

Please, leave a review for this book on Amazon

You can avoid being a victim by remembering one important rule: Banks generally will never ask for your information. If you absolutely have to make sure you need to update your account, contact your bank first.

To avoid these scams, stay updated with the latest phishing scam techniques. An updated browser and firewalls also help to prevent phishing scams.

There are also anti-phishing toolbars available online. These will alert you if you visit a suspicious website.

2. Protect your computer data

Defrauders can also get vital information about you by hacking your personal computer.

They can use a keylogger that records everything you type on your computer. They may also intercept your Internet traffic and record information you send online.

People who transact online are the most vulnerable to these kinds of attacks. But, there are various ways to safeguard your computer data from hackers.

You must use a firewall and set a password for your WiFi. You should also install reliable anti-malware software. Many hackers use malware and other viruses to get information from computers.

Also, make sure that you're using secured connections. Public WiFi connections aren't secured, so it's best to avoid using them as much as possible.

3. Protect your passwords

Using passwords is one of the ways that keep accounts safe. But, not using them properly would still make you vulnerable to identity theft.

Your password must be strong and not guessable. Shocking as it may seem, many people use "password" and "123456" as their passwords. These are actually the weakest passwords anybody could use.

Avoid using birthdays, phone numbers, or other personal information as your password. It's best to use a combination of numbers, letters, and symbols. In this way, your password will be difficult to crack.

However, highly-skilled hackers may still be able to get your password. Using multifactor authentication especially for online banking might add security to your accounts. Some banks, for example, require that you confirm a transaction by using a temporary pin sent to your registered phone number.

Please, leave a review for this book on Amazon

You must also have different passwords for different accounts. If one of your accounts gets hacked, all your other accounts would likely be vulnerable as well.

The most important thing to remember is to never share your passwords with anybody.

4. Protect your mail

Imagine all the information an identity thief could get from your mailbox.

Criminals do not only steal information online. They can also get your personal information from the mail you receive if they find a chance.

To avoid mail identity theft, start by cutting down the amount of junk mail you receive. This includes insurance and credit offers.

You should also keep mail with important information in a locked container. If your mail is piling up, you can shred them instead.

For incoming mail, you can either get a locking mailbox or a P.O. Box. The locking mailbox looks like a normal mailbox, but it can only be opened with a key. A P.O. Box may be safer than a locking mailbox, but you'll need to pay for it monthly.

For outgoing mail, you must avoid putting it in a mailbox especially if it contains checks or cash. Instead, drop it off at the post office or in a collection box. You may also hand it directly to a mail carrier.

But with today's technology, companies now offer paperless bills. This will not only prevent mail fraud, but you may also get some small bill discounts.

5. Protect your credit card number

As mentioned above, fraudsters can use your credit card to perform unauthorized purchases. All they need is your credit card number and your personal information.

The basics of securing your credit card start with your signature. Sign the back of your credit card as soon as you get it. Also, don't write and keep your pin in the same place where your card is.

Keep your credit card safe by not letting anyone in public see it. Sometimes, you may receive calls from your "bank". Unless you made the call, never give your card information.

You must also watch out for phishing scam e-mails from your bank. Even if it looks legit, don't give your personal details or credit card number.

It's also a good idea to update your bank information regularly. Update your phone numbers and e-mail address as soon as changes occur. Also, be up-to-date with fraud alert systems and respond immediately to notifications.

Please, leave a review for this book on Amazon

Lastly, report lost credit cards or any fraud activity suspicions right away. Your bank can block your account and credit card to avoid others using it.

6. Spot unauthorized credit card charges quickly

It's essential to check your credit card statements on a regular basis. Many unauthorized charges can go unnoticed for months if you don't do this.

Review your statements early and check for any purchases that you didn't make. If you don't report it ASAP, your credit card issuer will not give you much time to dispute. Also, you might end up being liable for the charges.

Call your issuer immediately once you spot an unauthorized charge on your account.

Once your credit score is tainted with a bad record, it's difficult to fix it. You may need to endure a negative credit score for some time before you can recover from it. Protect your personal information and educate yourself of the new scams criminals develop. Always remember that these criminals will never stop finding ways to get what they want.

We don't live in a perfect, crime-free world. You must be vigilant at all times to protect your interests. You don't have to fall victim to identity theft.

Did You Know?

Some banks offer secured credit cards to people with a poor credit history or no credit history at all. Secured cards can be the best option for your first credit card. The card is "secured" with a cash balance, a savings account, for example. You cannot touch this balance, or the card will be deactivated (turned off). If you charge over your limit, the bank can take the balance from your account. Your account acts like collateral for a loan. These cards may charge higher interest rates, but they offer the convenience of using a credit card while you build a good credit history.

Please, leave a review for this book on Amazon

Chapter 13

Do-It-Yourself Credit Repair Strategies

Bad credit can be such a bane to your finances, and any other related opportunities for that matter. A low score can prevent or hinder you from enjoying certain conveniences like being approved for loans or credit cards. You'll surely be exposed to higher borrowing rates as well.

Remember that your credit score is evaluated based on your financial information through the years. Creditors will take a look at your spending habits, especially those done on credit, and take note of how often you've borrowed money and what you spent it on. They will also take a look at your repayment history.

There are plenty of factors that go into your credit score. But don't fret because there are ways by which you can repair bad credit. There are easy-to-do strategies that you can consider to improve your score and open more opportunities in the financial market.

Now these strategies will be useful but they will take time, effort, and energy. But down the line, and provided that you do things right and maintain your new score, you can enjoy peace of mind and a ton of savings for your trouble.

Here are some of the simplest ones that you can do by yourself.

1. Get a copy of your credit reports for analysis and update your personal information.

One of the simplest ways to repair your credit is by updating your personal information. The funny thing about this is that it's so simple that a limited few recognize it as a viable strategy to solve this financial conundrum.

You might be wondering how outdated personal information can affect your credit score. Well, financial institutions use your records to determine your viability for loans and similar services. By constantly updating your personal information, you'll be giving them a clearer picture as to what your situation is in terms of work and finances.

Even if you update your information, your old details won't be erased or ignored whenever your line of credit is assessed. But any improvements in your professional and financial status will work wonders for your credit health.

It's important that you update your details and make sure that you monitor all of your credit information. Apart from seeing to it that all details possessed by your creditors are correct, doing so will also help prevent the onset of fraud and identity theft.

Remember that your name, job history, or addresses won't really be factored into how your credit is scored. But there are specific personal details that will be. These details will be extremely helpful especially if you decide to dispute your credit score.

When you update your information, you'll be able to remove any negative items, if any, that may be associated with old personal details. As these negative connotations are eliminated, you can expect your credit score to rise. But don't expect the process to be a quick one. When it comes to credit repair, patience is indeed going to be a virtue.

So how can you update your personal information? For starters, you can call your local credit bureau or find them online. Depending on the available service in your area, you might be able to do everything over the phone or computer. There are times when you might have to fax over some documents to start the process.

Surely you'll be working with multiple creditors for this so make sure that you provide the same information for all of the accounts that you'll be updating. Also remember to use the same format especially when it comes to names and titles. Be prepared as there are creditors that will require you to provide the necessary paperwork as proof of legitimacy before any changes are made to your accounts.

Keep in mind that you can request for your account information and current credit reports. Simply ask your creditors for these information. Review them and see where they may be any errors, typographical and the like. Take a look at addresses, employers, aliases, maiden names, telephone numbers, emails, and other details.

If you do spot any errors or see details that need to be updated, draft a letter requesting your specific changes. Double-check the information that you provide to ensure that there won't be any further mistakes. It will take the creditors several days to process your request so monitor them and follow-up whenever necessary.

2. Consider sending dispute letters to the appropriate agencies.

There are ways to get ahold of your credit report. Chapter 2 discussed this in great detail. Your credit report will include personal details and notable transactions from which your score is based. And it's not uncommon for people to discover errors in their respective reports; errors that serve to justify ratings that are less than desirable.

Once you get a hold of your credit report, take the time to review it line by line. See if there are mismatches in the information. See if there are typographical errors. Check everything so that you know with certainty that all the available information is correct.

Please, leave a review for this book on Amazon

If you find something questionable, or if you feel as if your credit score isn't justified, then give your creditors a call. You can also send them an email indicating your concerns. It will be good if you can fix everything here. But if not, do consider sending dispute letters to the concerned parties.

In this case, a dispute letter will serve to inform the creditor of any errors you've spotted in your report. You must indicate every one of them and provide the necessary correction. So make it a point to check what you've typed so that no further errors will be recorded.

You can then include a statement as to why you feel that your credit score should be reassessed or evaluated. If you've been paying debts off on-time and haven't missed payments then you should include things like these in your request.

The objective here is to make a strong case. So the more details and proofs you can provide, the better the potential outcome may be. And always remember to be polite. Have the proper attitude and your creditors will be more than willing to help you out. You can also see a guide on how to file a dispute with the credit bureau on Chapter 2.

3. Try your best to decrease your credit utilization.

If you take a closer look at your spending habits, can you identify where exactly you use the most amount of credit? Are you someone who borrows money for large purchases, say appliances, automotive needs, or for house payments? Or are you the kind of person who needs lines of credit for everyday expenses like shopping, utility bills, and the like?

There are some people who have bad credit scores because they overuse their credit cards or borrow money when they don't need the funds. If you realize that the same situation is applicable to you then it might be a good idea to minimize your use of your existing lines of credit.

What you should understand about credit scores is that they are not affected as much by how much you borrow on occasion but how well you repay these debts. Even if you borrow less and less money per month but pay on time and in full, if possible, then you can expect your credit score to improve.

In this case, take note of how much you regularly spend in any given month. This should cover your cash expenses, credit card charges, and existing loan payments. Then see where you can cut back on your credit utilization but give yourself enough time to adjust. Start with the small things. For example, try to use cash for groceries and utility bills. Do the same for when you do your shopping.

One of the best things about cash is that you can better manage your spending when you use it. Most of the time, people tend to overspend because they don't realize how much they're spending when a card is swiped at the register. Most of the time, they end up spending more than they can afford resulting to unpaid debts at the end of the month and a decline in their credit score.

Please, leave a review for this book on Amazon

Actually, if you can go all cash for your expenses then do it. Use your lines of credit for emergency purposes only or for larger purchases. For example, have a reserve credit card for unforeseen expenses. You can also have it on hand for the occasion when your cash on hand isn't enough for an important purchase. But be disciplined enough to use it for emergency purposes only.

Reserve your lines of credit for larger requirements. For example, use your lines of credit for home and automotive loans. Use the installment function of your credit card if you were to replace some appliances at home. You can also use it for medical expenses. But make sure that if you do, your monthly income is enough for you to meet your repayment requirements.

If you were to go this route, take enough time to help yourself adjust to the significant changes. Also have a positive and persistent attitude about it moving forward. Here is where personal discipline can have the most effect on the outcome that will come your way. Always think of the bright side – this can help you improve your credit score moving forward.

4. Add other lines of credit to your portfolio.

There are times when you may have the funds but not enough access to lines of credit. In this case, it will be a good idea for you to explore the idea of adding additional credit sources to your portfolio. As mentioned previously, credit scoring depends on your credit activity. So if you don't have enough of them in your history then you can expect a less-than-average mark on your record.

There are people who have gotten so used to using cash for various transactions that they end up missing out on a number of credit-related benefits. Even if they have the money, some of them find themselves in situations where borrowing, when needed, becomes more challenging than it has to be.

Keep in mind that even if you feel that you do not need a credit card, for example, it will be a good idea to have one or several in your possession. Even if you just use them sparingly, having these transactions can help improve your credit score over time.

But apart from credit cards, also consider taking advantage of larger borrowing opportunities if you have purchases that require such. For example, if you were in the market for a new car or home, even if you have enough cash on hand, getting a loan for these can be a good way to repair your credit score.

You might be wondering why you should consider spending on interest payments if you have cash for whatever it is you'll be buying. Well, for starters, there's such a thing as inflation. So the value of your cash now will be worth less as time passes. You will be at an advantage if you resorted to monthly payments instead of paying everything up front.

Please, leave a review for this book on Amazon

Next, by not utilizing most of your cash reserves, you're putting yourself in a situation where you are as liquid as possible. Surely there will be other more urgent spending requirements that will call for cash. When these arise, you can be sure that you have the necessary resources available and ready.

Thirdly, you need to have some form of borrowing history, both long and short-term, to have a basis for financial institutions to assess your credibility. They will look at your activity, repayment, and other factors as they determine your score. You want to have a good credit rating but without any substantial borrowing, it'll be quite difficult for financial institutions to come up with this figure.

So, take a look at your portfolio. Check out your existing lines of credit and, based on your spending needs, assess what other types of credit may be of use in the future. Do understand that you won't have to engage in a transaction to have additional lines of credit added to your account.

Simply call your preferred creditor and ask that you be granted an open line should you require it in the future. Surely, they'll be happy to oblige as this will mean that you'll have a larger propensity to use their service in the future.

6. Negotiate to have your credit limits increased.

When it comes to your line of credit, it's common to have multiple creditors offering different limits per account. Some institutions may offer you just the right amount to supplement your monthly needs while others may provide you with the kind of credit limit that can allow you to make large purchases month in and month out.

It would be an excellent idea if you reviewed your credit limits. This applies to all lines of credit from credit cards to loan provisions. Call your creditors and jot down the details. Having an idea of these figures will help you make better decisions when you borrow money moving forward.

There are different issues that borrowers commonly experience; one of them being mismanaged accounts. In this case, a borrower may tend to have multiple debts or loans that they lose track of month on month.

As a result, even if they have the funds, they miss timely payments and so on and so forth. Apart from added fees, their credit scores are affected by the regular onset of late payments.

One of the best ways to prevent this issue moving forward is by trying to see if you can get your creditors to increase your lines of credit. It's not just about having an ability to borrow more money but having the ability to just borrow from one or two creditors at a time.

By compressing your borrowing activities to one or two creditors, you can prevent missed or late payments as it will be easier to track your monthly obligations. As you're able to make the right payments on time, this will positively affect your credit score. It will also reduce the need to pay finance charges and late fees on your loans.

But there's another reason why you should work towards having your lines of credit increased. Having ready access to a more sizeable amount of funds can also mean that you will have more opportunities to run these credit lines.

For a lot of people, one of the reasons why they can't easily work towards repairing their credit scores is that they're not given as many opportunities to borrow money and therefore improve their credit histories. Basically, they're stuck with poor records as they can't show their creditors that they have developed the capacity and discipline required to be considered as good borrowers.

So if you find yourself in similar situations, it might be a good idea to call your creditors and have your accounts assessed for an increase in your credit limits. You can usually call it in or send a letter of request and then it will take the financial institution a few days to come up with an answer. Note that this can cause a small reduction in your credit score but its perks in credit utilization will allow you to recover those points and get even higher scores.

Some of them might ask you for additional paperwork for them to know more about your source of funds and monthly income. Don't hesitate to provide them with the necessary details as these can also be used to update your borrower's profile.

If there's something that you should be mindful of, it is that an increased credit limit doesn't mean that you have the luxury of spending even more money on loan. It doesn't give you that luxury. Always remember to still stick with a monthly budget.

7. Work on your monthly payment schedule.

Credit revolves around one main concept and that is borrowing money regardless of the purpose. And with borrowing comes the obligation of repayment. In this case, you should set your eyes on prompt repayment.

When you borrow money, you have to make sure that you pay the agreed-upon installments on time. Not only is this essential to keep your credit score at an ideal level but it will also help you keep interest charges at a minimum. Especially if you're in a situation where you can pay-off your debt in full, what reason is there for you not to?

Before you apply for any type of loan, be it a long or short-term debt, make sure that you're fully aware of the fine print. Read the details of the loan agreement so that you won't get any nasty surprises with regards to any charges later on.

Please, leave a review for this book on Amazon

Also, make it a point to ask as many questions as possible especially when it comes to the allowable payment terms. Depending on the amount that you plan on borrowing, you may be allowed a term of anywhere from three months to five years on average for a basic loan. And different credit institutions charge varying interest fees so shop around to find the best deal with the least amount of interest payable on the debt.

Before you sign anything, make sure that the monthly payable is something that you can live with. Depending on your financial situation and monthly expenses, you want an amount that's workable; one that you won't have a difficult time paying in full.

Include your monthly debt payables when you create your monthly budget. Make sure to set aside the money for payment as soon as you get it so that you won't end up using the funds on other things. Also jot down payment due dates. Especially if you have multiple debts that need to be paid, mark your calendar or set remainders on your phone or laptop so that you won't forget about any of them.

In this case, a good discipline will be to pay the debt days before the due date. If you find due dates that fall within the same range then do consider clustering them together. This way, you can do one or two bank runs in a month and have everything paid for on time.

This cannot be stressed enough but, as much as possible, pay on time and in full. When you pay on time, you eliminate additional finance charges and penalties from being added to your account. The same goes when you pay in full. Apart from these, you also enjoy the benefits of maintaining an excellent record with your creditors, which will then be reflected on your overall credit report.

As an added benefit, paying loans in full may even qualify you for better deals in terms of lower interest charges, waived annual fees on credit cards, and other perks. So try your best to practice a little bit of discipline and plan your monthly obligations out as best as you can.

You can do something as simple as updating your profile or requesting an increase in your credit limit. Or you can choose to go with something more complex and rework your spending and repayment strategies altogether. Whatever path you choose, know that either will lead to something beneficial – a potential improvement in your credit score over time.

You can choose to speak with your creditors over the phone or there are times when you might have to consider going the more formal route and send over an email or fax a letter. For the latter, you might also have to prepare some personal documents to help solidify your claims so make sure that you have immediate access to your financial records.

There are plenty of benefits that can be enjoyed by those with excellent credit scores so do your best to ensure that these conveniences will be extended to you by financial institutions. Now the strategies that have been mentioned here can stand on their own or you can choose to combine them.

Please, leave a review for this book on Amazon

Chapter 14

Biggest Credit Mistakes and How to Avoid Them

For many people, a credit card is merely a convenient way to make transactions. However, few people realize that the little plastic card also has the ability to wreak havoc on their lives if not used carefully. Ultimately, misusing your credit account can destroy your credit scores and ultimately hamper your credit.

One way to prevent the damages that poorly handled credit can cause is to know about the mistakes that people commonly make and learn how to avoid them.

1. **Paying just the minimum**

Issuers of credit cards set a minimum amount that you should pay every billing period. Some people have the wrong notion that this is a godsend because it is so small compared to the total amount. They couldn't be more wrong.

Paying just the minimum amount on your credit card debt will not only increase the time it takes to pay off your balance, but it would also accrue more interest. In addition, your credit score would suffer because as your balance grows, your credit utilization grows as well and that has a negative effect on your credit score.

To avoid having to pay more in the long run, try to pay the total balance every billing cycle. Don't let it accrue interest.

2. **Applying for too much credit**

If you are on the checkout line and the cashier asked if you want to apply for a store credit card for the discount, do not accept it outright.

You may love to have a discount on your purchases, but it is still a credit card. Remember that each time you apply for credit, an inquiry will show up on your credit report and will pull down your credit score a little. The discount you think you'll be getting might not be worth it.

Also, be careful about opening too many credit accounts if you plan on applying for big loans, such as mortgage, car loan, and others.

3. **Failure to report a lost or stolen credit card immediately**

Please, leave a review for this book on Amazon

The longer you take to file a report about your lost credit card, the longer the thief or the one who has gotten your card has to charge up your credit account.

If you immediately report your missing card before any false charges are made, the sooner you'll avoid possible responsibilities you have to deal with for the said charges. The sooner you report a missing credit card, the sooner it would limit your liabilities for false charges.

4. Ignoring Your Billing Statement

If you don't check your credit card's billing statement often, the more likely it is that you'll risk missing payment or paying less than you should have for it to be considered on time.

In addition, ignoring your card's statement will cause you to miss some important announcements, such as an announcement to the changes on your credit card's terms.

Make it a habit to check your billing statement because it will often be your guide to know if there are any false activities on your account. Besides, doing so will help you keep your spending in check.

To make sure that the payments have been correctly applied to your account, or if the all the charges are accurate, always check your card's billing statement.

5. Paying Late

Always pay for your monthly payments on time. If you keep on forgetting about your due dates, then you should come up with a system that can remind you about them. For example, you can set up auto pay with your bank or use apps to set reminders. If the primary reason is inconvenience, then organize your bills so you could schedule the best time to pay all if not most of them.

If you keep on paying late for your monthly payments, it can cost you for up to $38 in late fees, which will also depend on the number of times you have been late for the past 6 months.

Also, falling behind your payments for more than 30 days will also affect your credit score. But if your existing payment is more than 60 days late, then your card's issuer may raise your interest rate up to the penalty rate available.

6. Canceling Your Credit Card

Please, leave a review for this book on Amazon

Now that you have finally paid off all your credit card bills which have been stressing you out for ages, your first impulse might be to get rid of your credit card as soon as possible, which is usually done by cutting up your card and closing your account.

But don't be too quick on doing that, as closing down your account so suddenly can actually lower your credit score. Keep in mind that the age of your accounts affects your credit scores.

Even if you have paid off your credit card, it would be much better for you if you just leave your credit account open, that is until you are 100% sure that you can offset the possible reduction in credit score by making changes that would boost it. Just keep it open and maintain low utilization.

7. **Not Knowing Your Credit Card Terms**

If you know how your credit card company handles the late payments, you'll be more likely to pay for your card's bill on time. After all, you'll know exactly how much they cost you.

Also, knowing about the terms of your credit card enables you to have more control over your credit's costs. You will also know how you should or shouldn't use your card, which would be based on how your creditor will react to your actions.

That's why it's important to review the terms of your credit card at least once or twice a year. You can find them on your issuer's website, or request it from their customer service.

8. **Loaning your credit card**

When you loan your credit card to another person, you will no longer have control over the purchases that they are about to make.

In the end, you'll still be responsible for paying all the bills, even if the person who borrowed your card doesn't pay you for the expenses.

Never ever loan your card to someone, even if it's someone you know, except if you are prepared to take responsibility to pay for the purchases that they are about to make.

9. **Maxing your card out**

Utilizing more than 30% of your card's limit can be quite dangerous for your credit score. Also, by getting close to your credit's limit, it will put you at risk for fees that are over the limit, and even the penalty interest will increase your card's charges once you exceed your credit card's limit.

Please, leave a review for this book on Amazon

Therefore, to have a manageable payment amount and healthy credit score, always maintain a good credit card balance.

10. Letting your card get charged-off

Acquiring a charge-off is one of the worst things that can happen to your credit card report and credit score. A charge-off will remain on your report for 7 years, and could significant affect your ability to get loans and credit cards several years in the future.

It would take about a total of 6 months of missed payments for you to be charged with a charge-off status. Before your card gets to that point, ensure your delinquent accounts are current.

11. Sharing your credit card number with other people

Some credit card holders sometimes share their card's number to pay for a bill. But if someone calls, emails, or have mailed you with some requests and unsolicited personal information, such as your Social Security number or credit card number, never reveal it even if the person sounds legitimate or nice. These kinds of requests are part of financial scams that mostly target seniors. These fraudsters are trying to make unauthorized use of your good name and credit or steal your money.

If you do become a victim of identity theft, immediately report it to your Federal Trade Commission and to your local police department.

12. Getting pressured into accepting new cards

Have you ever noticed that sometimes most of the letters in your mail are about new credit card offers? Or maybe you have encountered countless strangers who are calling you to pitch you one? Well, don't think that these are just your imagination, because they are not.

A lot of credit card companies send out millions or even billions of credit offers every year, but this doesn't mean that you have to accept all of their requests or listen to their sale pitches. You can freely choose to get out of the prescribed credit card offers and out of the credit card telemarketing lists.

You can also get out of the email and phone solicitations from the mortgages companies.

Please, leave a review for this book on Amazon

13. Applying for credit repair recklessly

If you have recently gone through a serious personal setback such as a foreclosure, divorce, or bankruptcy, your credit standing might be shaky or maybe even downright bad.

However, looking for a quick fix can actually put you in the hands of a con artist that specializes on tricking people i.e. charge you with hidden costs or high upfront fees for their fake services.

Also, be aware of companies or an individual that promises to "fix" your bad credit overnight. Fixing a really bad credit score won't happen overnight, it lasts for days, weeks, or maybe even a month if the process is slow.

14. Paying tax bills with a credit card

If you don't pay for a federal tax debt, the IRS will have the power to tax your assets, put a right to claim or hold your property, or seize your tax refunds. However, none of it should intimidate you into paying them with your credit card.

The reason is that if you use your credit card, you will also have to pay for an interchange fee. This may run anywhere from 2% to 4% of the amount that you are paying for.

Now, add those to the 12% to 18% interest that you have to pay to your bank if you think of adding the tax charge to your balance. A better solution to your problem would be to set up a repayment plan with the IRS and pay your tax debts over time.

15. Aiming for the "rewards"

We people have been known to use credit for all kinds of things, be it a lavish vacation or jewelry, or even cars and in some cases, expensive novelty products.

However, making large purchases on a credit card is definitely a no-no unless you are 100% sure that you can immediately pay off such large amounts in full.

Whatever benefits that you may gain, in terms of flier miles or hotel check-ins, will come with interest charges, which you'll have to pay if you don't immediately pay your balance off every month.

16. Using your credit card to withdraw cash

Using credit cards to withdraw cash could be bad because the credit card issuer is not able to monitor the spending, and thus view it as a high-risk loan and subsequently charge higher interests.

If you don't fully pay off the amount you withdrew within a month, your balance will start racking up some interests. Therefore, you can quickly lose control over your debt if not handled as soon as possible, particularly if you only pay the minimum amount monthly.

17. Ignoring Your Credit's Warning Signals

To improve your chances of getting a healthy credit rating, check your credit reports for free for at least once or twice a year from a government-mandated website. However, if you're in the process of building or rebuilding credit, that isn't just enough. Check it once a month. You may also want to sign up for credit monitoring services, among others.

Also take note of warning signs that indicate you might be in a debt trouble such as missing payments, only making minimum payments, regularly seeking for 0% card offers, a low-rate balance transfer just to afford payments, or charging without knowing how to pay for bills.

If any of the following warning signals are familiar to you, it's time you get your act together to start repairing your credit.

Did You Know?

In 1996, the U.S. Supreme Court in Smiley vs. Citibank lifted restrictions on the amount of late penalty fees a credit card company could charge. Additional deregulation has allowed very high interest rates to be charged.

Please Kindly Review This Book

If you have found any value from reading this book, please kindly post a review letting us know

about it. It'll only take a minute of your time. Thank you so much!

Please, leave a review for this book on Amazon

Chapter 15

Start-up Funding Sources

Starting your own business does pose some of its own challenges. One of the biggest challenges you would face is amassing enough capital to fund your own business. Most starting business owners don't have that, unfortunately, which is why they look to other means of securing funding and other necessary resources.

There are multiple ways to do that and, for this chapter, we'd be looking at ten of them.

1. Bootstrapping Your Business

Basically, bootstrapping is starting a business with very little to no money. It also means you don't get help from angel investments or venture capital firms. What you do instead is plow back into your business the money you earn from your customers.

The 'bootstrap' word itself literally means getting into a situation using the resources in your possession. Generally, when you 'bootstrap', you are doing something difficult, on your own.

Don't get discouraged, though. A lot of businesses which have become successful started by bootstrapping.

Growing Your Money Through Bootstrapping

A bootstrapped business typically goes through these stages:

Seed money

You might start with your own personal savings, or perhaps a bit of financial help from family and friends. Just enough to get the business going. Some bootstrapped businesses even started as side business while their founders go to a regular day job. Then the founder somehow manages to save up enough money to grow the business.

Customer-funded money

Once you've started selling your services or products, you get in money from the customers. That money is then pumped back into the business. This keeps your business running which will also eventually fund the growth of the company. Growth in a bootstrapped business is usually slow. Initial funds are spent on operating expenses to keep the business running.

Please, leave a review for this book on Amazon

Loans and credits

Bootstrapping means you don't go out to get a big loan. Small loans may be required to fund some growth activities like hiring more people, evening out cash flow, or buying additional equipment. Credit becomes a secondary source of funds to keep the business operating and growing.

Pros and Cons of Bootstrapping

Bootstrapping has its own advantages and disadvantages. Here are some of them.

Pros

- **You answer only to yourself.** By funding your own business, you have full control. Businesses funded by VCs, accelerators, and angels are sometimes forced to give up equity and the fund sources themselves have their own particular interests, goals, and motivations which may not be aligned with yours. Bootstrapping gives you freedom wherein you can set your agenda and choose your directions.

- **You have focus.** Because there is little or no influence that can push your business into various directions, you can focus more on what your startup can do best – from bolstering the business' core competencies to coming up with flagship products.

- **You tend to innovate.** Necessity is said to be the mother of invention. And when you invest your own hard-earned money, necessity forces you to innovate. To invent and reinvent. Usually, because you have no other choice.

- **You become responsible.** When you own something, you tend to treat it with more care than if somebody else owns it. When you own 100 percent of the company, you'll be obsessed over the details of the business. This sense of ownership makes you more cautious and more practical in your decisions.

Cons

- **More need to generate revenue.** Because you used your own savings to fund your startup, it's essential to generate enough revenue to keep the business afloat. Early on, you need to have a successful profit plan that should be immediately operational. This necessity can result to growth paths that weren't in your original business plan. This can also hamper your growth.

- **Arrested development.** Because you don't usually have a large amount of money when you start up your business, developing key components that can fuel growth can be delayed. When you must invest part of the revenue on marketing, R&D, and hiring, you need to invest more time to plan else you'll bleed out money. Growth milestones may take more time achieve, and you'll just find yourself moving targets further.

Please, leave a review for this book on Amazon

- **Lack of connections.** In business, who you know can be as important as what you know. Other startup funding sources such as angels and crowdfunding can put you in the same room with people that open up potential markets and bolster valuable partnerships. This in turn gives you increased visibility. This is extremely difficult to do if you take the bootstrapping path.

- **Not enough credibility.** When you bootstrap, you are the only investor. Problem is, most customers will buy only from someone they know. Something that is easy if you have outside investors. Bootstrapping means you are the new kid on the block and people might think you're not credible. At least not yet. Credible investors give customers confidence to buy from you.

Basically, bootstrapping is the minimalist's approach to business. Minimalism is characterized by significant simplicity and sparseness. When you apply minimalism on your business, you're practicing bootstrapping. As much as possible, you avoid investing more money except when it's absolutely needed. You also need to work within your means and come up with ingenious ways to save money.

Bootstrapping might not be for everyone. It requires utmost discipline and restrain so that you don't go overboard when investing.

2. Crowdfunding

Basically, crowdfunding is a system of gaining business funds through collective efforts from individual investors, customers, family, and friends. Using this business approach, you can tap into these individuals via crowdfunding platforms and social media and leverage on their networks from wider reach and better exposure.

Crowdfunding is exactly the opposite of traditional business approach. With the latter, you need to do your business plan, prototypes, and market research. You then have to pitch the idea to large institutions or wealthy individuals to finance your project. Crowdfunding streamlines the traditional model because it gives the business owner a platform in building, showcasing, and sharing the pitch resources.

Types of Crowdfunding

There are several crowdfunding types or categories. What you choose as your crowdfunding method will depend on the service or product that you are offering as well as your development goals.

Please, leave a review for this book on Amazon

Donation-based crowdfunding

Basically, this type of crowdfunding means the contributors or investors are not expecting any financial return of their donations or investments. You can see a lot of donation-based crowdfunding activities like fundraising programs for medical bills, nonprofits, charities, and disaster relief.

Rewards-based crowdfunding

In a rewards-based crowdfunding system, the individual contributors to your business are offered a 'reward'. This reward is typically the service or product your business offers. Investors might be getting something in return for their investments, there's still no monetary or equity return so rewards-based crowdfunding is still considered a subset of donation-based crowdfunding. Indiegogo and Kickstarters are two of the more famous rewards-based crowdfunding platforms. They let business owners give incentives to their investors while avoiding extra expense or selling equity.

Equity-based crowdfunding

In an equity-based crowdfunding system, you allow contributors to become your business partners by giving them equity shares in return for their investment. As owners of your company's equity, these part-owners get a financial return or a share of the company's profits. This is given in the form of distribution or dividends.

Pros and Cons of Crowdfunding

Just like any other business approach, crowdfunding has some benefits and drawbacks.

Pros

- **It can save time and money.** Organizing a crowdfunding strategy is easy and fast. You don't need to do endless visits to private investors and banks.

- **You have access to capital.** Raising capital via crowdfunding usually takes less time that doing it by traditional means. A fundraising campaign is usually given a maximum of 90 days. This approach means constant negotiating, prospecting, and pitching is avoided which is the case when you get your funds from financial institutions. You don't even have to give your investors ownership of the business. You can do the rewards-based method instead. Also, there are no upfront fees that need to be paid.

- **Easy to establish a customer base.** Getting the first customers is usually the hardest part of a new business. But if you do it via crowdfunding, you already have a group of people interested in your offering. Through crowdfunding, many of the investors become both customers and an extension of your sales team if they promote your business. This business method also helps you in engaging with the customers.

Please, leave a review for this book on Amazon

- **You can organize a marketing strategy.** Crowdfunding is basically promoting your business idea to others while seeking funds to start it up. Once you get the funds required by your business to get off the ground, you already have an idea on how to improve your marketing strategy.

- **Control on how you reward investors.** Once you get funding, you alone determine how you'll reward the investors. You have complete control of how much interest or equity you offer to them.

Cons

- **No business-to-business offerings.** People who invest in a crowdfunding initiative identify with the offering or see its benefits. That's why most offerings are aimed at consumers and not to business entities.

- **Not for complex projects.** Crowdfunding works best if the business is simple. This approach will not benefit technical or complex projects because it won't be easy to make the investors understanding. Remember that these investors are mostly common folk. Projects that require long R&D cycles are not attractive to most people so crowdfunding isn't the best way.

- **Not for large fund businesses.** There may be exceptions but crowdfunding works best for projects that need less than $100,000 of capital. If your business idea will need a larger funding, you need to consider other financial sources to raise your capital like banks and other financial institutions.

- **All or nothing.** There are crowdfunding platforms that will only release the funding for your project once the campaign has reached 100 percent or more of the funding goal. If it failed to achieve the target, your funds can be stuck in limbo.

- **Makes the project inflexible.** Drastic offering changes on your project is not allowed if you've already received the funding. Timeline delays can also hurt your brand and damage your reputation.

3. Angel Investors

Basically, angel investors are wealthy individuals who provide financial assistance for a startup. Often, these investors expect ownership stake in the business. These investors are typically called 'angels' and would invest $25,000 up to $500,000 to assist a business in getting started. Oftentimes, these angels are the last resort for startup businesses if they're not qualified for bank financing or too small for venture capitalists (VCs) to be interested in.

Please, leave a review for this book on Amazon

VCs usually demand a quick return of investment but angels are more focused on the passion and commitment of the business founders as well as the wider market opportunity. This doesn't mean they're fine with losing money. They're just not interested in making a quick buck like VCs.

The 'angel' term was once used for wealthy individuals who saved Broadway productions from closing by investing in them. There were also patrons who supported creative professionals through financial means so these artists can focus on their work. The angels of today are modern-day sympathetic financiers.

What Angels Expect

Angels can make the difference between a business startup's closure or growth. But first and foremost, they are still investors. This means that they don't want to just give away their money. They will want it back after some time. That's why angels look for certain factors that will likely improve the odds that they will get their investment back.

Keep these factors in mind when you're pitching in front of an angel:

- Your track record and experience in the business
- The business plan's viability
- A service or product that's significantly innovative or disruptive
- Scalability of the business
- Current revenue
- Exit strategy

Pros and Cons of Angel Investors

Investing through angels is not a silver bullet that can solve all your business woes like a miracle. You need to know the pros and cons before you decide it's an appropriate investment method to explore.

Pros

- **It's great for small and medium size businesses**. The funding range of $25,000 to $500,000 make angel investment a great fit if your business is small or medium in size.

- **Open to high risk ventures.** It's a given fact that more than half of new business ventures fail before reaching the fifth year. This makes it difficult to get financial help from financial institutions and VCs. What makes angels great is that they're willing to invest in business that big banks won't want to get involved with because of the high stakes. Angels don't invest in the business but rather they invest in the founder. They have their sights focused on long-term goals. You don't get that from traditional lenders like banks.

- **Offers essential knowledge.** Angel investors offer essential experience and knowledge on the table. They usually work directly with business owners and help it achieve success. Their valuable assistance may include providing business strategy suggestions, expertise and guidance, and setting up the founders with potential clients. It's important to know beforehand if your angel investor may be able to help you grow your business.

- **Tax relief.** Capital-gains rollover is just one of the several tax reliefs offered by the US federal government to angel investors. By funnelling process to small businesses, the angels are able to deter capital gains on investments made. This law helps angels retain the investment and at the same time limit the losses if ever the venture fails.

- **Quick funds.** Capital from financial institutions needs considerable time to be processed and provided to your business while angels can give it almost immediately. This is important because time is of the essence when you are starting up a business

Cons

- **Funds may not be enough.** Angels are usually individuals investing their own money and are willing to take risks. To keep the risk within acceptable limits, they limit the funds they provide. This makes angel investment inappropriate for ventures that need large capital like energy or technology so you may need to look elsewhere.

- **Return of investment.** On average, angel investors will require around 25% of the profit made by the business. This may be too high for some business owners who are trying to grow their companies.

- **Can be difficult to work with.** Unlike financial institutions who are concerned only with the returns, angels are more involved with the businesses they put their money in. You may not desire that degree of involvement from your investors.

- **Difficult to pitch to.** Angels usually support more than one venture at a time so they have a lot of things in their minds. This might make it difficult for you to get your vision across during the pitching process.

- **They look for experienced business owners.** If this is your first business venture, it might be difficult to get financial support from angel investors. Angels usually look for experienced business owners who are able to provide positive projections of the business' success.

Given the advantages and disadvantages of an angel investment, it may or may not fit the vision you have for your business. Weigh each one carefully before you pitch in front of an angel.

Please, leave a review for this book on Amazon

4. Venture Capital

Venture Capital is a form of financing in which a starting business owner gets from financial institutions, lending companies, and even well-off strangers who have shown interest in the growth of the potential business. However, venture capital is not just all about money. It can even come in the form of technical/ managerial expertise as well as assets for use in the business.

On the perspective of the investor, venture capital deals are quite a gamble. However, the pay-off if everything is successful is equally huge or more.

The appeal of venture capital deals to starting businesses is quite apparent. For starters, most of their owners have yet to access capital markets. Also, they lack the expertise to effectively run the business which a venture capital provider might just be able to provide for.

Of course, this is not without its trade-off. To get funding, a business owner has to offer something in return which is always in the form of equity. To put it simply, if that business began or was intended to be a sole proprietorship, it has now become a partnership.

How It Works

The process of securing a venture capital deal can be straightforward. First, you'd have to find a venture capital firm who would look at your business plan and determine that it is both feasible in the short-term and sustainable in the long-term.

To do that, they will do a thorough investigation on every pertinent document you will submit. This includes income forecasts, the business model, a copy of the business plan, a timeline of the management and operating history (if already established, of course), and planned product/service line.

Alternatively, you can look for Angel Investors. They may be more lenient than a VC firm but you can be certain that they may ask for a larger equity in return.

Once the company deems your plan to be sustainable, they will pledge an investment of capital in exchange for equity in the company. The investment may be provided immediately in lump sum or in increments, depending on the investor. Either way, you should get the funding/assets you need out of the deal in the soonest time possible.

Please, leave a review for this book on Amazon

Pros and Cons of Venture Capital

Before you decide to apply for a venture capital deal, however, there are a few considerations you have to keep in mind.

The Pros:

- **Significant Resource Boost** - When it comes to resources, not a lot of deals out there can match what a VC deal can offer. Depending on the investor, you might get a gradual yet substantial boost in your capital or one massive spike.

- **No Financial Liability to Investors** - VC firms and angel investors are basically gambling away their money. If you succeed with the business, they succeed. If you don't, they lose a portion of their already sizeable disposable income. Either way, you are not obligated to pay them back if the business does not take off.

- **Networking** - Not every perk with venture capital deals has to be expressed financially or in tangible assets. With the right investor, you can get the expertise you need to run the business more efficiently. Also, these investors bring with them their own network of contacts, thereby increasing your own network as well as your visibility in the market.

The Cons:

- **Loss of Full Control** - Since you are adding in people to your business with their own skills, expertise, and money, you are effectively relinquishing full control over the business. Now, every decision you make has to go through thorough discussion before being executed. This means that every decision that the business makes is more carefully thought of. However, this comes at the expense of speed.

- **Clashing Goals and Priorities** - Investors and firms do not necessarily share the same goals you have with the business. They may want the business to take a direction which you wouldn't agree with or push things at a pace you'd find either too fast or slow for your tastes.

- **Managerial Distraction** - Remember the proverb "too many cooks spoil the broth?" One of the risks with adding in new investors to the business is exposing it to ideas that may not work to its best interest. If management gets too distracted analyzing what works best, the day-to-day operations might be affected severely.

Please, leave a review for this book on Amazon

5. Business Incubators and Accelerators

Aside from adequate funding, a startup business can also find a lot of advantages in having the right amount of outside support. It's often said that business models can be improved to maximize profits.

With that in mind, it is actually possible to give a business the facelift it needs right after or before it would be set up. And this is where business incubator and accelerator programs come into play.

Which is Which?

It's a common mistake to lump these two services together as if they are just the same thing. However, this could not be further from the truth as incubator and accelerator programs actually provide different perks to businesses.

Business Incubators

The goal of incubators is to provide business owners with the chance to come up with a better business right from the start. Things like office spaces, facilities, access to research data, and training are all provided by incubation centers. Such programs are provided by mostly business organizations, universities, non-profit groups, and government agencies and are generally directed towards starting business owners.

Business incubators are generally designed to get businesses set up in whatever industry they want to operate in as soon as possible. In some programs, funding may even be provided so that the owner can spend it on securing key assets and facilities for the business. Incubator centers can also focus on one industry such as technology, health care, and finance.

Business Accelerators

At a glance, accelerators offer seemingly the same services as incubator programs. However, as the name implies, these programs are all about speed. They are usually targeting entrepreneurs who already have an idea for a great business but have no means to translate those ideas into actual and profitable products.

How the work is actually more similar to that of Venture Capital. Investors look at your business idea and determine if it is feasible or not. Each investor has their own standard so what might be profitable for one accelerator investor might be different from another.

However, if they do find that your idea can work, they will then provide initial funding and training to help you set up your business. In return, they will ask for equity in the business. This means that they share creative control with you on how to run the business.

Please, leave a review for this book on Amazon

The entire goal of accelerator program is to help you come up with a startup and launch your own products and services in the market. That successful launch will then be used to pitch to other venture capitalists, giving your business a potentially massive influx of capital.

Pros And Cons of Business Incubators and Accelerators

As with any support service, support services like incubators and accelerators bring with them their own set of perks and drawbacks. Here are some of them:

The Pros

- **Being Part of a Collective** - When starting up a business, it often feels like it's you against everybody else. There are even instances when well-established businesses in a local area are threatened by the shinier, modern-looking newcomer.

Accelerators and incubators understand that starting up a business can be as isolating as it is difficult. As such, they primarily offer advice and guidance on how to set things right.

What you have to understand that these programs offer more than just funding. The technical and managerial expertise you will get is vital in making the business competitive and sustainable.

- **Instant Recognition** - The best thing that you can describe about accelerators and incubators is that they are, basically, crash courses in business management. Over a short period of time, you will receive education on the latest business trends and the training on how to apply them.

It also helps that some programs are quite well-known and certified in various industries which should help you secure funding. For instance, an investor might take a look at your business plan and notice that you have recently finished a course at a well-known accelerator/business program. That could speed up your applications for funding and make other investors less hesitant in doing business with you.

The Cons

- **They're Compulsory** - These programs are basically schools, which means that your attendance is more than necessary in some events. That time could have been otherwise used in more productive ventures such as improving on your business plan. Aside from being compulsory, the lessons you will attend might cover things that you as a business owner are already aware of or things that you might not find useful.

- **You'll Be Altering Your Plans, A Lot** - Although you do get connected to the network of these incubator/accelerator programs, that comes at the expense of you losing full control over the business. In most cases, the business plan/model you had before entering the program will not be the same when you leave it. However, you might consider these a small price to pay in ensuring that your business gets off the group as quickly as possible.

Please, leave a review for this book on Amazon

Conclusion

Understanding your credit is the first step to improving it. Hopefully, this book was able to help you do both. While there are now credit repair services, you may end up incurring debts to get them – so do be careful. Furthermore, getting such services will be useless if you don't understand how you landed a terrible credit situation in the first place.

You can improve your credit in many ways. As you learned from this book, it can be as simple as modifying your spending habits or correcting wrong information in your records. It could also be as difficult as paying all your debts at once and dealing with high interest rates. Don't forget to ditch the services that you thought would be helpful but turned out to be damaging to your finances and credit score.

Being mindful of your credit does a lot of wonders to your financial situation. It trains you to become a wise spender and keeps you away from personal bankruptcy. It also helps ensure that you won't incur debts that you can't handle. Above all, managing your credit will enable you to pursue the life you want.

It may take some time to see significant changes in your credit score. Nevertheless, you can feel some of its advantages as you keep on practicing good financial habits.

You'll need patience in enhancing your credit. After all, you're going to deal with different individuals and institutions in checking your records, correcting wrong information, and borrowing money.

The next step is to find and implement ways to increase your sources of income. You can do so by getting another job, setting up a business or investing. Make sure you have sources of both active and passive income. If you're interested in sources that will help you build passive income or just earn more money online, feel free to take a look at the second book in the Business and Money Series i.e. **Passive Income Ideas – 50 Ways to Make Money Online Analyzed.**

You may use a portion of your savings or credit to finance your new venture. With good credit score, you can get quick loan approval and low interest rate. Just keep in mind to pay your debts on time.

You're One-Of-A-Kind

In addition to everything, I would like to personally thank you for the dedication you've shown in reading this book to the end. That only shows that you are truly determined to create a better life for yourself.

It is a sad thing but the reality is that, once people start reading a book, they typically only read 10 percent of it before they give up or forget about it. Only 10 percent. What's terrible about this is that from this statistic, we can see that very few people actually follow through on what they commit to (at least when it comes to reading). The reason for this is harsh but understandable: most people are not willing to hold themselves accountable. People "want" and "want" all day, but very few actually have the fortitude to put in the work.

So what's my point? First, I am trying to tell you that if you're reading these words, you are a statistical anomaly (and I am grateful for you). But here's the kicker: in order to become successful as a result of this book, you are going to have to be in the .1 percent. You need to take action.

Set your goals and don't stop until you achieve them. Don't let anything or anyone try to discourage or bring you down. Just focus on those goals and keep on working and hustling towards them. That's what most successful entrepreneurs would do. Work hard, work smart, and be patient. These are the keys to achieving your goals. It doesn't matter if these are short-term or long-term goals.

I wish you the very best of luck!

Please, leave a review for this book on Amazon

www.ingramcontent.com/pod-product-compliance
Lightning Source LLC
Chambersburg PA
CBHW081443220526
45466CB00008B/2491